Early Literacy

Early Literacy:
The Empowerment of
Technology

Jean M. Casey

1997
Libraries Unlimited, Inc.
and Its Division
Teacher Ideas Press
Englewood, Colorado

Dedication

To Bill, Sean, Kevin, Chris, and Jenny for the stories and the love they have shared with me.

LIBRARIES UNLIMITED, INC.
and Its Division
Teacher Ideas Press
P.O. Box 6633
Englewood, CO 80155-6633
1-800-237-6124

Excerpt from the poem "Invitation" (Shel Silverstein, *Where the Sidewalk Ends*, Harper & Row, 1975) is reprinted with permission of HarperCollins Publishers. Copyright © 1974 by Evil Eye Music, Inc.

Library of Congress Cataloging-in-Publication Data

Casey, Jean Marie.
    Early literacy : the empowerment of technology / Jean M. Casey.
    xxi, 178 p. 19x26 cm.
    Includes bibliographical references and index.
    ISBN 1-56308-458-9
    1. Language arts (Early childhood)--Computer-assisted instruction.
  2. Reading (Early childood)--Computer-assisted instruction.
  3. Computers and literacy. 4. Educational technology.   I. Title.
LB1139.5.L35C37 1996
371.3'34--dc20   96-28987
                                                    CIP

Contents

Figures

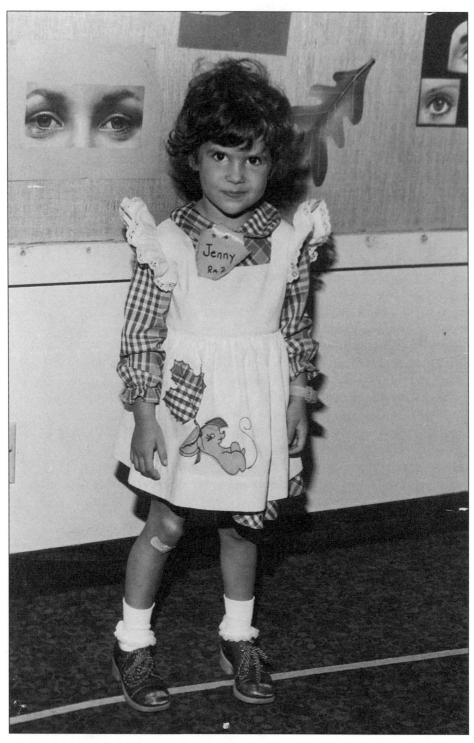

Five-year-old Jenny is bright-eyed and ready to start school. She has lots of stories to tell!

Foreword

Not since Apple put the desktop computer in the hands of children and Seymour Papert authored *Mindstorms* in the early 1980s has research been conducted on how the computer can free the human brain's potential for learning. Jean Casey writes that "three-to-six year olds are eager and willing to point the way." But the real question is, are teachers and the system of schooling as we know it willing to step out of the way? Are they eager to empower learners with the computer to make learning and teaching even more potent and allow children to lead the way?

Much was written about the promise and potential of computers at the onset of the last decade, but now, 15 years since computers were introduced into the schools, progress has been disappointing. Unfortunately, the computer is still widely used just as an electronic workbook. It's not that the technology has not advanced; it's just that the advanced technology that's available is underused, misused, or abused. We talk about authentic teaching and learning; computers and other technology also need to be used authentically so they become a seamless part of learning and teaching.

We must realize that teachers are no longer the sole source of information; children must be prepared to seek and acquire information on their own. Computer technology is, indeed, a powerful tool for discovery, learning, and self-growth. It is equally powerful in supporting the learning of writing and reading for all children. Indeed, it can level the learning field for *all* children, regardless of social, economic, or academic background.

This book explores parallel research conducted simultaneously by researchers in France, Spain, and the United States—at first unbeknownst to one another. All three researchers confirmed the importance of making available the technology of the "language machine," that is, word processing with voice capability, to free children to learn to write and read in ways that would astound conventional wisdom about emergent literacy. Through their work and case studies, they show how children empowered by technology can write and read in any language.

This book is required reading for all who have ever wondered about where technology will take our children. It will cause a shift in your thinking about how computers should be used in the classroom and at home. If you've ever been to Disneyland or Disney World, you know what an "E" ticket ride promises. Are you ready for an "E" ticket experience reading this book?

Julie M. T. Chan, Ed.D.
CompuKids Inc. and Coordinator
English-Language Arts/School Improvement
Orange County Department of Education, California

Preface

Children are the messengers we send to a future we shall never see.

Jonas Salk

I started out, as did most of the researchers in this book, in one of the most noble of occupations: Kindergarten/first-grade teacher. From the moment I began working with severely handicapped five year olds as a high school tutor, I was hooked. Hooked by the wonder of the five year olds, their honesty, their openness, their desire to be accepted, their intense desire to learn about everything. Most of all, I was hooked by that magical moment when they look at you with great excitement and say, "I can read!" Maria Montessori called the young child's learning process the Absorbent Mind. What a pleasure to witness the absorption process. I am continually in awe at how easily most young children learn language and then write and read in spite of—not because of—all the reading approaches we throw at them. Working with five year olds raised many questions for me throughout my 36-year career. Why did most of them never easily make that transition from oral language to written language? What was needed to help them? All wanted to be literate and to succeed. What was going wrong, and what could we do to help?

For 14 years I have been researching the effect of computers (specifically the talking computer, or a computer with word processing and synthesized speech capabilities) on the literacy development of young children. I have evaluated thousands of kindergarten and first-grade children's writing samples, created with and without the computer. I have worked with children on many types of computers with many types of talking software. Most of my research was in the California area, although the IBM Writing to Read sites I visited were scattered throughout the United States. My research and classroom work with large numbers of young children convinced me of the efficacy and power of a talking computer during beginning literacy. I have gathered stories written by the children I have worked with in many classrooms. I use these stories to express ideas and to illustrate the truth of learning in the words of children.

Dr. Laura Meyers of the University of Southern California, one of the first researchers in the field of talking computers, was my mentor. Her focus as a linguist and a speech teacher was on 3–4 year olds who had damaged vocal cords and could not communicate. Her prime concern was to help these children communicate with the people that loved them. Dedicated to finding a solution, she looked at the possibilities computers offered. She designed a special keyboard to provide easy access for the children, and she designed the appropriate software (KeyTalk). She must have looked with great pride on the success of the children and their parents. Through communication made possible by Dr. Meyers's knowledge and efforts, their bond was strengthened.

As a student of Dr. Meyers and as a reading specialist, I was concerned about young children who do not learn to read. Extending Dr. Meyers's ideas, I did my research on the average five and six year olds in kindergarten or first grade. I found another colleague in the United States who shared my belief in the power of the talking computer in early literacy. This was Dr. Maria Gonzalez-Baker. Dr. Baker has done outstanding work developing Spanish literacy software and using this talking software to support the early literacy development of Hispanic youngsters throughout the United States and Puerto Rico. Some of her work is reported in this book.

Last year, I was invited to present my ideas to the European Schools Project Conference in Cambridge, England. I looked forward to sharing ideas with European educators. At this conference I met Dr. Rachel Cohen from University Paris–Nord. Dr. Cohen, a brilliant leader in the early childhood field, had been doing research similar to mine for many years. She has written seven books on the subject, authored many articles, and given many speeches. Two schools in Spain are named for her. She pioneered the use of the voice synthesizer in the discovery of the written language by young children. When we listened to each other present our research, we each found a kindred soul. Dr. Cohen told me of the work of her friend and colleague, Dr. Gloria Medrano, who is conducting similar research with computers and young children in Spain. The circle widened.

I knew an overwhelming body of evidence indicates the computer is a very powerful early literacy tool, but at that conference I realized the global impact of all researchers' combined work. What we had all discovered—in various parts of the world with children speaking various languages—was that the success we had achieved in fostering early literacy was not particular to a culture or language, but rather a universal development. All children, regardless of language or culture, can be supported and empowered by the use of technology during their early literacy development. Most important, technology allows children to learn much earlier and much more effectively than earlier researchers ever believed they could. In the process of searching and asking questions about how technology can nudge or foster the developing early literacy of young children, researchers discovered lots of other things about how young human beings learn.

I owe thanks to all these fellow researchers who have shared their work with me and the hundreds of kindergarten and first-grade teachers who have worked with me over the past 14 years. However my biggest thanks goes to Codey, who was the first five and a half year old who showed me the light. Working on an early 1980s Apple IIe, Codey found the success that turned an occupant of the Buzzard reading group into an author right before my eyes. I wanted to tell every educator what Codey had taught me about literacy, about success and self-esteem, and about the tools we write with. Here was a word processor for children, a machine that, with just a simple touch of a key, created a professional printout of a letter or word and then a life story. A machine that could take a child's language experience story from his fingers, turn it into print, and read it back to him. A machine that empowered a young child to write his own message without relying on an adult to transcribe it. I had witnessed Codey work on the language machine, and his writings were what 14 years later I would call language processing. That's the story I have to tell.

This book is for educators, teachers, and administrators. It is for student teachers and graduate education students. It explains the sound qualitative research and years of observational research that has been done around the world on the use of computers with young children.

This book will increase your observational skills and make you question the quantitative tests that have been used for so long to mismeasure young children and stifle their true learning. As Stephan Jay Gould says, in *Mismeasure of Man*, "We pass through this world but once. Few tragedies can be more extensive than the stunting of life, few injustices deeper than the denial of an opportunity to strive or even to hope, by a limit imposed from without, but falsely identified as lying within" (Gould 1981). Scores on standardized tests of reading and language arts can devastate a child's hope to be literate by imposing arbitrary limits. It is far better to assess children by the learning we observe and the oral wisdom they share through their writing. Like Michelangelo freeing a statue from within a block of marble, educators must recognize the fantastic capabilities of the developing human mind and foster its unfolding, rather than test it and put it away in a small box. Each of the educators you will read about in this book, when told a child could not do something, asked, "Why not?"

This book shares messages of children from all over the world who have experienced success with the language machine. They are the writers and readers of the twenty-first century.

Chapter 1 presents current research and writings about what we have learned so far pertaining to literacy and how children learn to speak, write, read, and function in the culture they were born to. Chapter 2 gives a brief history of how the language machine was developed and how researchers discovered that typed print frees the children to write. The results of children and teachers working with this tool are presented. Chapter 3 shares Dr. Rachel Cohen's innovative work with computers and young children in France and illustrates the similarities in childrens' learning across cultures. Chapter 4 presents the research of Dr. Gloria Medrano and Dr. Maria Luisa Herrero Nivela, of the University of Zaragoza, Spain. Their research pertains to the use of computers with three year olds and presents some innovative discoveries about using a computer corner for young children. Chapter 5 describes the conclusive work done using computers with special needs youngsters, showing this technology is essential to their learning. Chapter 6 discusses the Writing to Read program and its implementation and effects on classrooms across the United States. Chapter 7 introduces other literacy programs, like the Apple Early Literacy Connections Program, KidWorks 2, SABES and SESOS (bilingual Spanish/English literacy programs). Chapter 7 also includes sections on adolescent and adult literacy programs. Chapter 8 is a very important one for the classroom teacher, for it describes how computers can be implemented in the classroom. Chapter 9 describes a sample qualitative evaluation that is a model for schools to use when evaluating technology programs. Chapter 10 discusses the problems involved in changing the culture of schools. Chapter 11 discusses future directions of technology in our classrooms and how, if used properly, it will empower learners.

It is important to note that use of the computer is not the sole solution to all educational problems. But it is an effective tool that can engage and empower learners, especially those who have not felt either engaged or empowered in classrooms before.

Introduction

Codey in Los Angeles, California; David in Santa Maria, California; Raoul in Paris; Fernando in Huesca, Spain; and Laurel in Sydney, Australia. What do all these elementary students have in common? All of them, along with a significant portion of other learners throughout the world, have learned to communicate using the spoken word but have failed in their attempts to develop their communications abilities using the written word. They can see, hear, understand, and speak well; but when they sit down at a desk with a pencil, they do not achieve the success their peers do. Some respond by breaking the offending pencil; some find solace under the desk; some amuse themselves by distracting others; and some stare out the classroom window as if looking for escape. Some scurry around the classroom like a nervous animal, looking for ways to be amused or successful, yet they always end up back in their seat with a pencil and worksheet and another opportunity to fail. It doesn't take long for them to figure out they must be dumb. Some develop a stomachache, some demonstrate such unacceptable classroom behavior they are given all sorts of labels (attention deficit disorder and learning disability are just two labels). Predictably, regardless of culture, gender, or age, there is damage to their self-esteem. This damage further inhibits their ability to learn to write and read in their language, for if you believe you cannot write and read successfully, you won't. A cycle of failure has begun. Visit a classroom anywhere in the world, and you can spot the learners in this predicament.

This book brings together research conducted separately around the world in an effort to find ways to help learners in their early writing and reading acquisition stages. Dr. Jean Casey in California, Dr. Maria Gonzalez-Baker in Texas, Dr. Rachel Cohen in Paris, and Dr. Gloria Medrano and Dr. Maria Luisa Herrero Nivela in Huesca, Spain, bring together their research, which attests to the facts that the need for early literacy is a global need, and the empowerment of technology in helping young children is not an isolated phenomenon. Wherever educators have worked with children and technology, regardless of the language, the early literacy development replicated itself over and over again. Educators, parents, administrators, and all those working with early literacy learners will find this information important in developing their own school early literacy programs or in working with specific learners.

The book is also appropriate for teacher training classes and in-service teacher training seminars. The information it provides for implementing technology in a school and providing an environment to foster this new way of learning is important for school administrators and researchers involved in restructuring schools. Changing the culture of schools and empowering young learners through the use of technology is a major undertaking. As with any innovation, the first response is to adapt it to our comfortable teaching strategies. However, just as we have discovered that it would be foolish to warm a dish on the stove before placing it in the microwave, so we must learn new ways to handle technology that conform to the unique characteristics of the technology. As difficult as it has been to find the funds in education to provide sufficient access to technology for all learners, a greater problem has been bringing the knowledge to educators to see how this technology is most effectively used in the early literacy process.

In the field of second language acquisition, Dr. Stephen Krashen writes about a possible "affective filter" that limits input. If this filter is "up," no matter how beautifully the input is sequenced, no matter how meaningful and communicative the exercise is intended to be, little or no acquisition will take place (Krashen 1981). This important theory helps us to understand second language learners' reluctance to risk using a new language once they have failed at it or been laughed at for mispronunciation. Secondary and adult learners who have never used computers suffer from this same "affective filter" syndrome. Because these attitudes are so powerful, learners must be offered learning opportunities before the filter falls into place.

A significant number of educators in the schools think children at age five or six cannot write. These educators believe the young children are somehow intrinsically not ready to write. Rather than allowing these children to try to write, adults take dictation and write for the children or recopy the child's text directly on the child's paper, convincing the child he or she is not ready or cannot yet write. Problems of penmanship—as distinct from writing, or creating text—obscured the issue for all the years that the pencil was our primary tool for written communication. However, the scene has rapidly changed today, with the advent of the talking word processor. What we have discovered over the past 14 years of using this technology with early learners is that they indeed have the thoughts and ideas, and it was the eye–hand coordination that hampered them. Empowered by the keyboard where they can effortlessly produce a professional-looking letter, word, sentence, or story, they are able to put their thoughts and words on paper. Of course, their first efforts may consist of their name and the names of everyone in their family, words they see in the classroom or in meaningful print (all can spell Disneyland). With encouragement from educators, they soon pick up the words they need to express their thoughts. The professional printout they are able to create daily, which proves their authorship, is so motivating that their output explodes. This works for all children—those with advanced eye–hand coordination and—equally important—those who lack that coordination. A great proportion of the students who are labeled dyslexic and end up in special education classes worldwide have as their root difficulty an inability to express or read ideas in print. The talking word processor—that is, a word processor that incorporates synthesized speech—opens the world of print to such students.

It is the author's hope that educators will embrace the talking word processor to open the world of print to all learners in the early stages of literacy regardless of age, learning ability or style, culture, or language.

Chapter 1

The New Literacy

If you are a dreamer, come in,
If you are a dreamer, a wisher, a liar,
A hope-er, a pray-er, a magic bean buyer…
If you're a pretender, come sit by my fire
For we have some flax-golden tales to spin.
Come in!
Come in!

"Invitation," Shel Silverstein

We all have stories to tell. Some, like the storyteller, can weave a tale that entrances us; some, like the writer, can spellbind us with the flourish of a pen. Others can do neither of these things. Tim, a five year old in an archdiocese of Los Angeles classroom, is autistic, and Codey, a five year old in a public school across town, cannot handle a pencil or pen. How can they tell us their story? How can they be heard?

> It is the children who have difficulty learning to read and write alongside their peers that are most often at risk in our schools. Delays and difficulties in learning to read and write are the most common reasons given for retaining children, labeling them, placing them in a special track, group, class, or program. In the schools we have, children who do not experience early school success too often experience no success at all (Allington 1996).

What you are about to read will show you a new way of communication that has opened a window and shown us a key. The window is the computer monitor, and the key is the keyboard. Together, they have made it possible for those who have been silent for many reasons to tell us their story. They make early school success possible for students who once would have been doomed to failure at age five.

Children from all over the world have the following basic needs:
to be accepted,
to be respected,
to learn,
to be self-actualizing,
to communicate,
to be like their parents or adults they know,
to be independent, and
to experience success.
If the classroom environment can bring all those things to every child, then we have
succeeded in helping all to achieve literacy.

Joining the Literacy Club

Learning, I propose, is primarily a social rather than an individual accomplishment. We learn from other people, not so much through conscious emulation
as by "joining the club" of people we see ourselves as being like, and by being
helped to engage in their activities. Usually we are not even aware that we are
learning. One of the most important communities any individual can join is
the "literacy club," because membership ensures that individuals learn how to
read and write, and because reading is the entrance to many other clubs
(Smith 1988a).

Literacy has been defined as the ability to read and write (Cooper 1993). However, if
we look back in time, we can see that it has not always been defined that way. For a
Sumerian child, the measure of literacy may have been the ability to read and write on
clay tablets; for a child of the jungle, the measures of literacy may have been the abilities
to read the tracks of animals hunted by the group and to write the symbols representing
the day's kill.

Various cultural groups require various forms of literacy. To be considered literate
by a social group, one must perform reading and writing skills in ways acceptable to
that group. Each time and each culture has required messages for adults to decipher
and understand. Western European-based cultures, for example, have recorded messages with pencils, pens, and print. For the child living in the cosmopolitan global
cities of the twenty-first century, writing and reading will be accomplished using a
machine (computer) that displays characters that are input by typing or by speaking
to the machine. Books will be read, but some narrative materials will speak, as the
Children's CD-ROM Living Books by Broderbund do.

There is hardly a service in our world today that does not rely on a computer for
some aspect of its operation. Gordon Wells states that to be fully literate is to have the
disposition to engage appropriately with texts of various types in order to empower
action, feeling, and thinking in the context of purposeful social activity (Wells 1986).
Frank Smith, the noted educator and writer, says we learn to read by reading and to
write by writing (Smith 1988a). Smith's observation can be expanded to include writing *with the tools of the society we live in*—that is, the computer.

Children freely learn their spoken language from the earliest stages. Helping them to identify and clarify the conventions of print is as necessary as helping them to depend on meaning and the larger structures of language. There is a place for planned instruction, but such instruction will be emulative and invitational rather than pre-scriptive. It will support and not supplant the learning system of each learner, and will express itself in respect and trust for the divergent ways in which children teach themselves the tasks they wish to master (Holdaway 1979).

Children learn to listen, speak, write, read and think by having real opportunities to do these things. Literacy develops in real-life settings for real-life activities in order to "get things done." Children are doing critical cognitive work in literacy development during the years between birth to age six. Literacy develops as students encounter many authentic or real literacy experiences. Children learn written language through active engagement with their world. They interact socially with adults in writing and reading situations; they explore print on their own; and they profit from modeling of literacy by significant adults, particularly their parents (Teale 1986). This is what happens when all goes well. But what about children who have difficulty with early written language? Helping children to overcome this difficulty is the central responsibility and challenge of the school and of a common-sense community. The responsibility for early failure can never be shifted onto the shoulders of failing children. The major causes of failure in the great literacy undertaking are not to be found in the incompetence of children, but in the departure from the sound educational principles of developmental learning.

Millions of children have developmentally learned to speak their native tongues since time immemorial (Holdaway 1979). Given this knowledge, how do we view the child who has the desire to learn and the opportunity to write but who lacks the eye–hand coordination to make anything but scratches on paper? Educators must look for alternative ways to help these children achieve early literacy success.

Educators know that some classroom procedures and paper-and-pencil tasks inter-fere with students' developing literacy. However, the response to students' failure has been to put them in special education, remedial, ADD, special day, low group, slow group, or some other "box." Students who are boxed and labeled know what is expected of them; they are expected to stay in their box. Thus, failure becomes a self-fulfilling prophecy. For these students, the tools of learning are not the only burden they bear; the damage to their self-concept is a major block to their literacy development. Thus, educators' first job in trying to undo the damage is to change the students' attitude about their ability to learn.

Once children have the basic ingredients for early literacy:

- a positive attitude toward writing and reading what they have written,
- listening to adults reading to them, and
- being surrounded by interesting books,

then they need the final ingredient: time to read, read, read.

In *The Power of Reading*, Stephen Krashen (1993) posits that free voluntary reading (FVR)—that is, reading because you want to—is missing in many school programs. Free voluntary reading means reading what you choose, because you are interested or need information. It means no book report, no questions at the end of the chapter, no looking up every vocabulary word. It means putting down a book you don't like and choosing another one instead. This is the kind of reading highly literate people do obsessively. Krashen concludes that, if children or less literate adults start reading for pleasure, their reading comprehension will improve, their writing style will improve, and their spelling and grammar will improve. He found that, when children read for pleasure and get "hooked on books," they effortlessly acquire language skills.

The Technology Solution Begins Early

Katie is finishing her first letter to Santa Claus. There is nothing unusual about that—except that, at three years old, she is writing her letter on a laptop computer and sending it to Santa via the Internet! Will, age two, loves to play with the Macintosh keyboard and The Playroom software. He is learning numbers and colors, and he talks about what he is doing all the time. He is developing his language ability at the same time he is subliminally picking up visual, spatial concepts and knowledge.

In the United States, the average age of children who start to use computers at home is 18–24 months (Public Broadcasting System 1994). Generally, parents provide the same risk-free environment for computer learning that they provide for language learning, that is, excitement about and praise for the child's curiosity, attempts, and success. Children are as fearless exploring the keyboard as they are exploring other exciting parts of their environment. Because no one has told them they cannot succeed, young children are much more willing to use and experiment with the new technology than are adult learners who, after years of failure, are reluctant to risk failure.

Children's absorbent minds reach their peak for learning multiple languages between the ages of 18 months and 7 years. Computer language is a language like any other. Thus, the peak time to learn computer language is the early years. Studies of the brain, as well as ethnographic observations, support this observation.

Technology and Literacy Development: A Brief History

Studying the effect of technology on early literacy is a recent endeavor. Early research began in 1983. Researchers like Dr. Laura Meyers at the University of Southern California, were pioneers in the field. Meyers developed a software program called KeyTalk. It was accessed by a special membrane keyboard. Instead of having keys like a normal keyboard, this membrane keyboard had pictures that were laminated and placed over sensors. Children pressed the pictures instead of keys. KeyTalk was specifically designed to test whether a talking computer (that is, a computer with synthesized speech capability) could help nonvocal three and four year olds (most suffering from damaged vocal cords) to communicate with their parents. The capability for synthesized speech was achieved using a speech card and an Echo speaker, both installed on an Apple IIe machine. Using this machine, parents and children held their first verbal conversations.

Much of the success of KeyTalk owed to the fact that the child controlled the output. Earlier software used digitized speech (a vocabulary of preprogrammed words that children could choose from). This earlier software required children to communicate within the confines of a programmer's agenda. Unlike this earlier software, KeyTalk empowered young children to develop their own written language in the same way children develop their spoken language: through trial, approximation, receiving praise, and understanding. Meyers's work, featured in *Smithsonian* magazine, sparked interest in what would come to be a very powerful learning tool.

Integrating Technology in the Classroom

The printing press had an enormous impact on storytelling and oral traditions. The computer is having an equally significant impact on print materials. Meaningful integration of technology into the learning environment is appropriate. Individually innovative teachers around the world have been researching the use of computers in the classroom; however, widespread use of technology in the classroom has been extremely slow in developing.

Early Efforts: The 1980s

In the 1980s, Seymour Papert's *Mindstorms* (1980) and his LOGO software caused a flurry of interest in the potential of the computer as a tool to teach geometric concepts. Workshops were held, articles written, and kits and materials to support the LOGO program designed. However, rapidly changing technology rendered classroom machines obsolete much more quickly than school budgets recognized the need for upgrades. This problem caused the whirlwind interest in LOGO to wane. Nevertheless, over the years, the software has been improved and developed to work with the latest hardware, and it continues to be one of the finest available learning tools for mathematics.

One valuable lesson learned from research into how children used LOGO to learn mathematical concepts is that, when used as a problem-solving tool with the student in control, the computer can be a very effective learning tool.

In the reading and language arts curricular area, the available software was often modeled after workbook exercises in basal series. It resembled the "drill and kill" method of teaching more than the constructivist or child-controlled method. Some innovative educators recognized the pitfalls of this approach. In *Microcomputers: The Promise or the Threat*, Frank Smith states that, if computers are used merely as "drill and kill" delivery systems, it would be better not to use them at all (Smith 1984).

Large companies introduced Instructional Delivery Systems (IDS) based on behavioral lesson design. These systems attempted to teach reading and language arts skills through multiple-choice exercises. Students rapidly lost interest in reading short paragraphs and then answering one multiple-choice question after another. Even computers are boring under these conditions!

In the late 1980s, John Henry Martin developed an early learning program by linking the latest knowledge of reading development to Moore's research into the power of the talking typewriter. Moore's research (Moore 1961) had been largely ignored by the education community. Moore and other researchers had concluded that it was much easier for children to create letters by tapping keys rather than by arduously recreating the traditional Palmer method's three-inch-high letters on dotted templates. These researchers realized that the printing we require of young children has more to do with calligraphy than with communication. (To exacerbate matters, we require this expertise in printing before children's small-muscle coordination has developed!)

Martin called his program Writing to Read; he sold it to IBM for $1 million. The program is now used by thousands of children in more than 36 states of the United States.

The Age of Computers

As we approach the twenty-first century, we are seeing an explosion in the number of personal computers in homes as well as in schools. Thirty-four percent of the people in the United States have computers in their homes, and the number increases daily (Bilotti 1996). (It should be noted this figure refers to the *total* population of the United States, not the school-age population. The portion of the student population with computers in the home is somewhat less than 34 percent.) Children who live in homes with computers are fearless when it comes to playing with them and using them to learn. As software improves, observations of how the computer can empower young children to learn steadily increases.

There are some basic criteria that parents, as the first teachers, and educators must keep in mind when promoting this new learning tool. The computer is best used as a tool to aid thinking and writing and is especially powerful when the user controls the learning.

Piazza and Riggs's observations of kindergartners use of the computer to explore written language reveal that, in many ways, their explorations involving the computer are like those involving pencil and paper. However, because the computer offers a unique stimulus for writing, children were observed to experiment with speech and writing in ways specific to the machine. For example, Piazza and Riggs's story of a kindergarten child named Selen shows how the child used the machine to play with oral and written speech. Selen creatively combined chanting and letter experimentation as she worked at the computer. She spoke to the computer in ways reminiscent of the language adults use when they are playing games in which they wish to control the action. This opportunity to become engaged in word processing and keyboard functions allows young children to explore language in new, computer-specific ways. "This language play facilitates children's systematic organization of print, their formulating and testing of language hypotheses, and the stimulation and development of symbolic thought" (Piazza and Riggs 1984).

Perhaps the term *inventive spelling* is deceptive; one teacher calls this type of spelling *transitional spelling*, and perhaps that term is more accurate. Inventive spelling is the intuitive spelling students use during early written language acquisition, especially in English, because many words' spelling does not match their sound. Examples of inventive spelling include *wuz* (was), *thu* (the, one of the most common words of the English language), and *skool* (school). Just as we accept and acknowledge spoken language approximation (as when a baby says *baba* for bottle), so we accept the written approximation of speech. Through teachers' modeling of standard spelling and through daily exposure to literature, students acquire the correct English spelling and begin to use it in their daily writing. To facilitate the process of acquiring correct spelling, it is essential that the adult refrain from correcting or crossing out inventive spelling; rather, the adult should accept the meaningful message, get excited by the message, and encourage children to expand on their written ideas.

When children are encouraged to use inventive spelling, the following words appear in their stories:

difrunt	Sindrelu	perte	ryflacshin	atinchion
publisht	cwolebere	chilljrin	hontit	icsplode
hosbitle	inemore	Kintuke	evree wun	
invitashin	magicl	emedetly	swolod	
skreching	aspechle	groj	naber	
cuple	ruf	doter	extermnator	

All the above words are from stories by five year olds. Notice the descriptive words, like *perte*, and the complex words, like *ryflacshin*. Considering that these words are part of children's listening and speaking vocabularies when they come to school, imagine how boring the "Mat ran, Pat ran, Rat ran" stories of preprimers must be. Basal readers with controlled vocabulary are an insult to early literacy learners at any age. All learners need to learn to write and read using the language they own.

Because our own early writings were subjected to rigid correction, many adults do not understand the concept of not correcting early writing attempts. Only by observing how children really learn and by reflecting on how damaging early correction has been throughout one's own writing experience can one come to this understanding. (Even our leaders do not understand the importance of inventive spelling. In his education pronouncement for the year, the governor of a very large western state vowed he will not allow the teaching of inventive spelling. His statement reveals his misunderstanding of the process of acquiring written literacy and shows how far educators have to go in helping adults understand the process.)

Sample of Early Descriptive Language

I have a   gerbil.
Some times he bits my thumb.   Alvin
is growing up. 3 days after cristmas
he will be 2. I cant wait.   That is
the first pet I ever had.
I might get another pet. Some times
when I pick him up he droops at both
ends and some times he falls out of your hand.

Story by a first-grade student

Notice the description of the gerbil drooping at both ends. The exaggerated spaces between words indicate this learner has noticed how space exists in print. Note the knowledge of content, syntax, and grammar this first-grader displays.

Literature and the Computer

The daily reading of good literature to children daily is essential to a literacy program. Many children will want to re-read for themselves a book a teacher or peer shared orally with the class. After hearing a pattern story such as *Rosie's Walk* by Pat Hutchins, one child went to the computer and wrote the following story:

A turtl .   went across   A pond.he met a duck. the duck   took a   walk
with the turtl   then   they met a hen.   The hen took a walk with the turtl
and the duck.   Then they   met a cat. then they went up a hill. then they
went down the hill.then they were lost.

Written by a first-grade student

Writing daily not only helps literacy development but can help social and emotional development as well. For years, humans have been writing in journals, trying to put down thoughts and feelings and solve personal dilemmas through writing. Following is a personal dilemma of a first-grade student. Without daily writing at the computer, the teacher would not have been aware this incident bothered the student.

One day I was mad at my teacher. She said that I stood up on the merry go round at recess & I did not. Susan did. I got really mad. I have not talked to her since. One day she came up to me I turned away. She said, " Kelly this has been going on long enough. Sheri told me that she really stood on the merry go round " good" I said.Well could we forgive and forget?Sure.On my way hom I wondered what forgive and forget meant.When I finally arrived home I went and asked my mom what it meant.She said it meant to firgive somebody & forget what they did.Well I forgave her and everything is back to normal.

Written by a first-grade student

Some critics fear computers will bring about isolation in learning; however, studies have shown that not only can preschool children engage in cooperative problem solving and instruction, but technology can stimulate social interaction in problem solving.

Researchers have worked with three year olds using the computers for exploring music and art. In both music and graphic arts, the computer allows children of any age to explore, discover, and compose. It creates an environment in which every person is creative—and knows it (Clements 1985).

The use of the computer supports Piaget's view of learning. According to Ferreiro and Teberosky's explanation of Piaget's view of learning,

the concept of learning, (understood as the process of obtaining knowledge) inherent to genetic psychology rests on the assumption that there are learning processes that do not depend on methods.... A method may help or hinder, facilitate or complicate, but not create learning. Obtaining knowledge is a result of the learner's own activity. An intellectually active learner does not necessarily carry out observable activities. An active learner compares, excludes, orders, categorizes, reformulates, confirms, forms hypotheses, and reorganizes through internalized action (thought) or through effective action. A learner who carries something out according to instructions or a model provided by someone else is not, usually, an intellectually active learner (Ferreiro and Teberosky 1989).

Used effectively as a tool to aid writing and thinking, the computer enables young children to turn their thoughts into print, which they can read, rethink, and revise. It also allows them to effectively demonstrate the literacy they own.

Figure 1.1 tells a story about a boy named Codey. In the past, Codey's literacy development would have been evaluated based on his drawing. The drawing shows rudimentary eye–hand coordination and small muscle control. Measured by the Gesell Developmental Scales (Gesell 1940), the circles Codey used to draw the man are figures a three year old would draw. The large head with no body is characteristic of a very immature beginning drawing and indicates Codey's lack of motor control. Based on the drawing alone, one might conclude that Codey is quite immature. In the past, Codey might have been assigned to the low reading group, based on his drawing ability.

Codey   2-14-96

It is raning hrd twoda. I lik the
ran bekaz I lik gateng wet. I lik
plaing in the ran.

Figure 1.1   Codey's story and drawing

In *The Child from Five to Ten*, Gesell and Ilg (1946) state that a five year old can write just a few letters of his name, while an eight year old can write several sentences. What would you expect of Codey's writing, based on his drawing and on Gesell and Ilg's statement?

Now contrast the drawing with what Codey wrote using the computer. He understands phonics, for he has the correct sounds to construct meaningful words. He understands syntax and semantics. He can write descriptive sentences using many parts of speech. He understands capitalization and punctuation. His story has a beginning, middle, and end. He conveys his feelings about the rain to the reader. He writes several sentences, so by Gesell's standards, he writes like an eight year old! Suddenly, Codey appears to be a quite intelligent first grader. Obviously, it's important to distinguish between intelligence and motor skills.

Given the many benefits of the computer for early learning, equity is a very important issue in early literacy. The opportunity to use technology for the writing process must be available to all. Children who do not have computers at home must be able to use them at school and after school, in libraries or community centers.

The Long Road to Understanding How Literacy Occurs

As we examine future learning and the new ways we have to help children in their early literacy development, it might be useful to explore how researchers have learned from one another and how we have arrived at the level of understanding we have today. Suffice it to say that, although children usually construct their own language in five years, it has taken a century of research and observation in education to provide a glimmer of knowledge about how children actually achieve this and how we might aid, rather than interfere with, their development of written, telecommunicated, visual, and oral literacy.

At What Age Should Children Be Taught to Read?

Many schools still work with entry criteria that were established by a 1931 study by Mabel Morphett and Carelton Washburn. After testing 141 children in Winnetka, Illinois, Morphett and Washburn concluded "it pays to postpone beginning reading until a child has attained a mental age of six years and six months" (Morphett and Washburn 1931). Acceptance of this notion prompted publishers to develop many readiness tests, including some still used today, like the Metropolitan Readiness Test. It's important to note that this entire industry of testing, readiness materials, and curriculum development rests on the foundation of a single 141-child Illinois sample as well as the notions that children must be ready for the "curriculum" that was to be done unto them and they are not ready to read until they have their six-year molars and a mental age of 6.5 years.

Today we know that infants learn from birth, and very rapidly. We know many three, four, and five year olds write, use computer keyboards and VCRs, play video games, and read children's books. Nevertheless, the age of entry to first grade remains 6 years, and many educators still operate as if that is the magic hour we should begin to "teach reading"—as if no learning occurs until we start to expound on the sound of the "short letter a."

Early Attempts to Improve Learning: Kindergarten Screening

In 1976, I wrote my master's thesis on prekindergarten screening. The idea for my research came from a school principal, Dr. Patrick Monahan, who loved children and was disturbed by the fact that some children failed the Metropolitan Readiness Test and so failed before they even began school. The purpose of the prekindergarten screening was to assess the abilities of five year olds to perform some of the skills that would be required of them in school. Parents of children who were deemed not ready to begin school were advised to take their child (usually a boy) home for a year and hug him.

Again, though this procedure was fraught with good intentions, the notion that the curriculum drives learning and children may or may not be ready for it to be bestowed on them was problematic. Screening procedures, such as the Gesell tests of writing and Draw a Man, were used to judge the child's intelligence and readiness for school. (Gesell had published scales that included age level norms for the amount of detail included in the Draw-a-Man.) We never considered that what we really might be testing was eye–hand coordination rather than intelligence.

This is not to say that all screening is bad. Screening young children for vision, hearing, or other physical difficulties certainly is beneficial, because the earlier they receive assistance in these areas the less the difficulty will interfere with their learning and success in the classroom.

The Institution of Readiness Testing

The belief in readiness, as was and still is institutionalized by some schools and publishers, implies that reading instruction can only begin efficiently when children have mastered a basic set of skills. It implies that composing and other aspects of writing (except for letter formation, or handwriting) should be delayed until children learn to read (Teale 1986).

Building on this idea, publishers raced to develop scope and sequence charts of readiness and reading skills. They created reams of criterion-referenced worksheets for teachers to teach each skill and periodic formal testing to assess each skill. Suddenly classrooms contained shelves and shelves of prescriptive materials designed to deliver instruction in a sequence, much like building a car. The materials came with the publishers' assurance that children who mastered every step of the scope and sequence chart were sure to become readers.

This notion of learning lasted longer than 50 years. It created the impression that early childhood behaviors were only previews to the "real" reading or writing taught at school. Perhaps what was wrong with this notion was the focus on the child as deficient for the ideal school environment. Perhaps, as Sylvia Ashton Warner, discovered in her work with Maori children in New Zealand, the key is to focus on the learner and develop the curriculum for their interests and needs, instead of the other way around (Warner 1986).

Fortunately, the observations of Margaret Mead and other anthropologists shed light on children's learning in many cultures. Psycholinguists, such as Chomsky, Holdaway, Smith, Goodman, studied language acquisition, and this research found that children are constructors of language. Subsequent research found a parallel between language acquisition and written language proficiency.

Marie Clay was a pioneer in examining young children's reading and writing in light of language acquisition research (Clay 1991). Her research and writings have caused primary teachers to look at children's learning behavior in new ways. Her method has been one of careful observation of how children learn to read, and her focus has been on issues of prevention and ways in which problems may be overcome before they are firmly established. She was greatly influenced by Dolores Durkin's studies of early readers (Durkin 1966). Durkin studied the children of professors at the University of Illinois; these children were reading before they entered school. Based on her research, Durkin described the process by which early readers learn to read on their own before they enter school without being taught but rather by being read to, by observing adults as readers, by observing meaningful print, by pretending to read books, and finally by reading the ones they choose and love. Durkin showed that children learn writing and reading in a manner parallel to their language acquisition. Her work became a landmark, much quoted study.

Interestingly enough, some years later, Durkin said, "The publishers have misconstrued my research that said some children read early due to the kind of literacy experiences they have had in their home environment to meaning that all children should learn to read in kindergarten. Now they are selling schools Kindergarten textbooks to teach reading. The worst part of it is that they support the use of these materials, workbooks, and tests in the name of my research! That isn't what I said at all!"

Based on Durkin's work, publishers concluded they should create materials to teach all children to read at age 5. However, Durkin's findings do not imply that because many children learn to read on their own, educators should suddenly force-feed all children. Rather, we should take our cue from successful learners and provide support and an environment that will help them construct their literacy at their own pace.

Summary

In the past decade, researchers have found the speech-enhanced word processor plays a key role in aiding the development of written literacy, thus helping to prevent early failure. Now, it is up to educators to provide equal opportunity for all young children. The word processor can be used to empower young children; regardless of the language they speak or where they live. It can be universally successful.

Chapter 2

Birth of the
Language Machine

Across the world children have entered a passionate and enduring love affair with the computer.... Large numbers of children see the computer as "theirs"—as something that belongs to them, to their generation.

Papert 1993

Early Research in Aiding Literacy

More than 50,000 hours of research has been done on the use of the typewriter and the talking typewriter with young children (Moore 1961). This research has largely been ignored. Moore documented dramatic stories of two, three, and four year olds using automated and manual typewriters to learn to read. His major purpose was not to demonstrate what had been known for a long time, that young children can and do learn to read, but to develop a theory of problem solving and social interaction. Most interesting, he had a child who had some experience with his program introduce a new child to the typewriter. He then left the new child alone to explore the typewriter. In exploring it, the child would strike a key, and the automated typewriter would call out the name of the letter. Thus the child would learn the names of the letters and punctuation symbols and be in control of the learning. Next the children viewed words or symbols on a screen similar to a television and reproduced the letters on the electric typewriter. Soon the children were typing words and sentences and reading them. Moore was ahead of his time. He discovered that, given the tool—a typewriter—children could learn to read much earlier than expected. He stated it is not necessary to wait until children are six years of age before starting to help them to read. Furthermore, Moore said, many of the factors considered essential for success in beginning reading really are unessential.

The best time to start reading, according to Moore, is at age two or three, when the child is still free to explore, when learning is a game, and when the child is not upset by failure. The most important readiness factors are the ability to sit, speak, and listen to a natural language (Chall 1983).

Initial Teaching Alphabet

During the same period of time, in England, Sir James Pitman created the Initial Teaching Alphabet (ITA; Pitman 1963). Recognizing that English spelling is extremely irregular and thus very difficult to learn, Pitman augmented the 26 alphabet letters with 44 symbols that correspond with the sounds of the language. Under Pitman's program, children learned ITA-style reading and writing in first grade; in the second grade, they transition to the traditional alphabet. My son, Kevin was in first grade in an experimental ITA class at Branch School at Edwards Air Force Base in California. At the time, I was teaching first grade at the same school, using Economy phonic series. Thus, while I was following the manual to teach the short *a* sound to my students, Kevin and his classmates were writing long stories in what looked like a foreign language. Kevin's teacher proudly shared long-language-experience stories written by the children; in contrast, my first-graders could barely write short phrases or copy one sentence out of the Economy workbook. We were all amazed. The problems occurred in second grade, when the children were told, "the rest of the United States uses 26 letters, so we want you to forget the 44 letters we taught you and use these 26 letters!" In many cases, it was harder for children to relearn the alphabet; many children left the experimental program confused. Not all children had trouble making the transition.

Although in the United States, Albert J. Mazurkiewicz and Harold J. Tanyzer published a series of books called the *Early to Read: i/t/a Program*, the ITA method did not catch on. Still, Pitman was right about the difficulty of the spelling task in our language and he did in fact show that, when given a means to write sounds, children can be successful. For some students, like Kevin, the ability to write long stories using ITA provided a springboard for later writing.

In most schools, children who do not learn under the school's established reading method are placed in special education. The number of children in these classes continues to grow. In special education, the search for devices to assist in communication has always been a concern; and much of our educational technology reflects that search.

Language Experience as a Predecessor to Language Processing

To understand what a significant breakthrough this was in the learning of reading, we must go back to the 1960s when Dr. Roach Van Allen created a reading program called Language Experience (Van Allen 1976). Dr. Van Allen had spent his career working with children, trying to discover why some learned to read easily while others did not. He discovered what became the cornerstone of his method; what a child could say, he could write; what he could write, he could read. This was the missing link to reading success. Rather than present beginning learners with text foreign to their experience or have them struggle to understand other author's meaning, the first step was to help learners realize the words they could already speak, when written down, became the words they (and others) could read. This was a vital connection, one that gave students motivation to read. It is based on the human tendency to be interested in stories about ourselves.

Many educators agreed with Van Allen's notion that learners need to be interested in print and to make the connection between the spoken word and print to become readers. The Language Experience Approach (LEA) began to gain in popularity and appear in classrooms. The method worked—where there was one teacher for every two children. The method relied on each child dictating a story from his or her own experience as an adult recorded the story on paper. The child then read back what he or she had just dictated. With classrooms of 25–30 students, teachers soon found themselves running around the room to record each child's words. Many exhausted teachers, even those who saw the potential of this approach, in desperation fell back upon the basal reader and preprinted materials; they traded relevance for convenience and ease of use. Even the hearty souls who persisted with the Language Experience Approach were unaware of the subliminal message they were sending. The message was: You can speak and dictate a story, but you can't write yet. Only the teacher (or an adult) can do that. Without realizing it, teachers were delaying children's early literacy by assuming they could not write or read. What we failed to consider was the possibility that it was the writing tool (pencil) itself that was hampering early writing–reading connections.

The Language Experience Approach did not die. Reading specialists, special education teachers, and adult literacy instructors all recognized that when working one-on-one or with a small group in teaching beginning literacy, having each learner tell his or her story and then read it aloud is one of the most powerful methods for helping learners construct their own reading and writing system. However, until the birth of the language machine, this approach was used only in limited fashion. Basal reader instruction; skills-based, criterion-referenced reading programs; and phonics programs were the most popular classroom reading programs in the classroom.

Today, the potential for speech synthesis and recognition programs seems limitless. What better way to teach children (or adults) to read than to add speech to what they type or to add "typing" to what they say? Here we have all the advantages of the Language Experience Approach and word processing with voice-over added (Strickland 1987)!

A Simple Talking Word Processor

Laura Meyers's early work with 3–4-year-old, language-delayed youngsters inspired her to try using a computer with additional components—graphics and speech—to elicit speech and communication. Her first research was carried out using an Apple IIe computer with a special membrane keyboard designed for easy access, and an Echo speech synthesizer for sound. She developed the Programs for Early Acquisition of Language (PEAL) software. This program centered on pictures representing the most common objects and words in the young child's vocabulary. Her success with this program led her to develop, along with Terri Rosegrant, an Arizona educator, a simple talking word processor. This software for the talking word processor, called Talking Textwriter, was soon purchased by Scholastic and marketed as Talking Screen Textwriter Program (TSTP). The IBM version was called Listen to Learn.

At this time, I was using TSTP in my research at the University of Southern California while completing my Ph.D. I decided to use a model similar to the one Meyers had used with 3–4-year-olds; however, my population was average kindergarten students in various stages of early literacy. The TSTP software and the Apple IIe with the Echo speech synthesizer worked well. However, installing the sound card often was a difficult task for teachers.

Synthesized Speech

In 1982, I visited a small software-development company, First Byte, in Long Beach, California, to see whether it would be interested supporting my research into the use of a talking computer with early literacy learners. As it happened, the president of the software division, Mary Cron, was hoping to develop a talking word processor using SmoothTalker, a new speech software designed by First Byte. SmoothTalker was the first computer program that contained synthesized speech on a disk that worked with a Macintosh computer. This innovative technology required only a 3¼-inch floppy disk to make the Mac speak! No speech board to cautiously install; no risk of burning up the motherboard. No extra speaker to carry around or lose. All that was needed to turn the Mac into a talking computer was the SmoothTalker disk.

The software program designed to work with SmoothTalker, called KidTalk, was tested on elementary school populations. KidTalk was a talking word processor designed to be used by the very young. It proved to be a very powerful tool. It permitted children to write whatever they wanted and also to select a male or female voice to read their writing back. Students could adjust the speed, pitch, and volume of the spoken word; they enjoyed playing with intonation and the prosodic elements of language. Using KidTalk, children could type conversations and have them read back in human-sounding voices; this contributed to the children's ability to experiment and play with language, oral and written, in early developmental stages. KidTalk could also repeat letters, words, sentences, or the entire text, based on the child's selection. The ability to hear letters read back contributed to beginning alphabet recognition. The ability to hear a sentence read back aided development of syntax. Listening to the entire story contributed to the child's sense of story and meaningful learning. Developed by a reading specialist and teacher, this program was designed and extensively tested with children.

The distinction between synthesized and prerecorded speech is important. Synthesized speech is the cornerstone of the talking word processor. During the 1980s, the public was used to the concept of digitized speech or prerecorded speech put on computer disks to speak words the programmer had prerecorded. Digitized speech was a powerful addition to the auditory output of computers, but listening over and over to "This is a cat" can get as boring as reading, "Dick ran, Jane ran, they all ran." So, the educational potential was limited to teaching, "This is a cat." However, the development of synthesized speech, or the converting of digital information into sound waves that humans recognize as speech, was a major breakthrough. This method, in contrast to the recording of sound and storing it in digital form so the computer could reproduce the recorded message, involved teaching the computer how to create speech. In the text-to-speech system, the computer reads—that is, speaks—the text that is typed into the machine (Casey 1985).

THE BENEFITS OF UNLIMITED SPEECH OUTPUT IN THE LEARNING ENVIRONMENT

1. It can help children hear and understand the sound patterns of English as they use talking computer tools to read, speak, and write.

2. It motivates children to write. Writing becomes an interactive and dynamic form of expression when children hear their text immediately read back to them.

   Text-to-speech output can be controlled by the children, allowing them to hear their texts as often as necessary. This eliminates the negative experience of repeatedly asking for a teacher's help to make the program work or to understand the words on the screen.

3. It allows children to read and write English before they have mastered the mechanics of literacy, such as letter names and sight vocabulary. If they have trouble reading a word, they can direct the computer to say the word. In this way, the computer acts as a decoder.

4. Speech coupled with visual display helps focus the children's attention on the language activity.

5. It provides the necessary auditory component in the learning environment. The children can hear, see, and touch information about written language.

6. It increases creativity and skill in written self-expression as children hear and critique their own written work. With the speech component, even very young children can become active, creative writers.

7. It allows even young children to be autonomous learners able to master program operation through spoken instructions and help messages.

8. It allows a high degree of personalization by incorporating spoken reinforcement messages customized for each child.

9. It can be a voice for children who have difficulty speaking. Children with language disabilities can learn to write sentences before they speak them; seeing the text and hearing it spoken improves their oral language skills.

10. It provides audio validation for menu selections and program operation for visually impaired users.

11. It makes it possible for children to change word pronunciation and make the connection between how words sound, in contrast to how they are spelled. (English, despite its complexity, can be reduced to about 50 discreet sounds, called phonemes. Text-to-speech systems break text into phonetic building blocks, then pronounce those building blocks in units that more or less resemble words. Early versions of text-to-speech required an interface board and speech chip to run.)

SmoothTalker was the breakthrough Macintosh product that provided text-to-speech capability on a disk without the use of additional boards or speakers. The problem was that SmoothTalker was ahead of its time. It required a 128K Macintosh computer, and it wouldn't work with the Apple II computers that were in the classrooms at the time. Nevertheless, the technology was available for students to record their thoughts and experiences using a keyboard, see their words on the screen, hear their words read by the computer, read their words along with the computer, and print what they had created. Language processing was born!

(Eventually, First Byte was purchased by Davidson Software Associates. Davidson expanded the product, adding phenomenal graphic capabilities that allowed children to add pictures to their story. But, as sometimes happens with project replication or program acquisition, Davidson eliminated some of KidTalk's most valuable literacy learning capabilities, including two-voice dialogue, changing the prosodic elements of speech, and reading back individual letters. These capabilities need to be included in any literacy learning tool.)

Problems of Past Reading Programs

In the 1970s and 1980s, kindergarten and first-grade teachers had many popular reading programs to choose from. One was a reading program that used a linguistic approach with text like "Mat sat on a fat hat" to teach reading. Hoping that Mat's experiences on a hat would somehow capture the interest of young learners more than Dick and Jane had been able to do with their controlled vocabulary, the authors of the series contrived stories around word families. What educators discovered was that many children learn to write and read in spite of—not because of—the current fad or method or approach employed. Regardless of the success teachers had with some children, there were always students who did not "get it." Jeanne Chall, of Harvard University, called them the ones "who fell through the educational crack" (Chall 1983). They were the students who struggled and did not learn to read; soon they either silently gave up or acted out or hid under their desk, or earned a reputation for being a problem. Unfortunately, educators did not recognize all those behaviors as signs of frustration with the lack of literacy success.

Phonics

Publishers advertised phonics-based materials as if they had found a panacea for reading success. In reality, students who were truly hooked on phonics often had great difficulty reading complete words; they felt compelled to sound out each letter of a word first; worst of all, after laboriously sounding each letter, they still had no clue to its meaning. Not even a glimmer of comprehension, the sounds for *kuh-ah-tah* bear small resemblance to the *cat*. Still, phonic approaches sold. Kindergarten teachers would proudly point to letter charts circling their rooms, use their long pointers to point to each isolated letter and, like drill sergeants, lead their small charges in isolated repetition of sounds (*b*, buh-buh-buh). My favorite was "whirling blender, whirling blender, bull, bull, bull" for the *bl* sound. The children repeated the phrase with the precision of a Marine platoon. The teacher proudly smiled as they completed the z sound and sat down. Once again, the students had mastered the isolated sounds but made no connection between those sounds and the words they spoke or read.

Many beginning reading programs confounded children instead of helping them construct written language for themselves.

The Search for New Solutions

During the 1980s, educators began to look beyond the research of the behaviorists, who had been education's major source of information, to researchers in the fields of anthropology, sociology, linguistics, psychology, and education. At a 1982 symposium in British Columbia, researchers from Europe, North America, and South America came together to talk about how young children, rich or poor, from all parts of the world, learn. They agreed on three points:

1. All children learn constantly, without special incentives and reinforcement.

2. Children learn what is done by the people around them.

3. Children learn what makes sense to them (Smith 1988b).

The computer as a literacy tool seems to fit in with all three of those points. Children learn constantly; they are not afraid to explore and to risk using a new tool (a keyboard) to write. Daily, children see people around them, from their parents to the cashier at McDonalds, using computers. When children themselves use computers in their learning, for the first time they have the power to create letters and words, to hear their own words read to them, and to print their words to keep and to show others. The computer empowers early learners and this, indeed, helps their learning make sense to them.

Lessons from Students Who Learn to Write and Read a New Way

Codey's Silverfish Count

Codey was the first to teach me important lessons about the various ways children learn and how technology can turn them into authors on the first day of school. Codey was a five-and-a-half-year-old boy I taught using Talking Screen Textwriter software and an Apple IIe computer when I was completing my Ph.D. at the University of Southern California. I was doing research to find alternate methods of teaching for children who were not learning to read using standard approaches.

When the kindergarten teacher brought Codey to my group, she informed me he was one of her low, low students. She said this in his presence, as if he did not have ears to hear or feelings to feel. Codey came to me with a hurtful label, a label so damaging it inhibited his future success. In his heart and mind, Codey believed what the adults around him had been saying: He was dumb and could not read. Watching his peers, who were successful writers and beginning readers, confirmed Codey's suspicion that he indeed was different. He was stupid. With this belief as his foundation, everything Codey attempted turned out poorly and reconfirmed his negative self-image. Soon he stopped trying. Before he knew it, he was in the lowest reading group, a group made up of students who had determined one way or the other that they were failures in reading and writing.

When I met Codey, the first thing I noticed about him were his downcast eyes; his reluctance to experience another teaching event; and his negative body language, complete with stooped shoulders and the slow walk of someone who believes he is a failure.

The first task I gave to the students was to tell me about their pets. Codey amazed me with his outstanding oral language development as he related that he had "a cat, a dog, a turtle, six goldfish, and 100 silverfish." I decided there was quite a bit of intelligence hiding behind Codey's reluctant brown eyes. The next task, however, easily accomplished by most of the children, was the key to Codey's classroom woes. I asked the students to copy the sentence they had dictated to me. (I had written each sentence on an experience chart.) Codey held the large kindergarten pencil and stared at the lines on the paper. He looked up at his sentence and, as if not to disappoint me, made a valiant attempt to copy the letters. No matter how hard he tried, the lines didn't turn out right. Soon he was erasing everything on the paper. A large hole appeared in the paper, and then he dropped his pencil. This allowed him a few moments of escape as he groped about under the desk. In his seat again, trying to master the pencil strokes, he hit his hand upon his forehead in abject frustration. As he watched the sentences appear on his peers' papers and heard the teacher's praise they each received, he once again was reminded of how really dumb he knew he was. He retreated under a desk. "Codey, sit up in your chair right now or you will have to put your name on the board." As the teacher's voice floated to him, he realized he couldn't hide or escape from this school failure, no matter how hard he tried.

However I had something he had never used before, a computer. He saw adults using them, but no one had let him touch one. I called him over to the computer. I had already put his name in a file. When I told him to hit "control t", he easily struck the two keys. He saw his name, Codey, appear on the screen and heard the computer say his name. He smiled. "Can it say anything else?" he inquired. "What would you like it to say?" I asked. "Can it say, 'E.T. phone home'?" "Sure, go ahead and put that in." Slowly, Codey found the keys he needed to write E.T. fon hom (his inventive spelling). When he hit the appropriate key and heard his sentence read to him, a huge grin covered his face and his eyes lit up with excitement. He wrote about Pacman and his family. Each time he added something and listened to his own language read back to him, he beamed. Next, I told him to hit "control p." He did, and his story printed. I showed him the paper copy and said, "This is your story, Codey, read it!" "You know I can't read," he replied. "I don't know that," I said. "You read what you wrote on the computer screen, didn't you?" "Yes, but that was different." Paper represented failure to Codey. I took the paper and held it in front of the computer screen. "This says the same thing," I said. "Try it." Hesitantly at first, he tried and slowly read "Codey ... E.T. fon hom." As the words came out, he picked up speed and a big smile broke out on his face. "I can read," he shouted. "Can I have that paper to show everyone?" He walked out of the room with his head held high, body straight and moving fast. I realized that Codey's categorization as a low-level student in the elementary classroom had been erroneously based on his lack of eye–hand coordination. With a more sophisticated writing tool, he was able to demonstrate the knowledge he already had.

Dyslexic Nicholas: The Heavy Label

Nicholas was coming to the remedial reading clinic at the university. He was flunking, and his parents were frantic. In the clinic, reading clinicians worked one hour each week with children labeled remedial readers. I trained the clinicians, or tutors.

Nicholas's tutor came to me distressed. She said she had been trying all the ideas we spoke about in class but they were not working with Nicholas. I agreed to work with him at the next session while Rose observed through a two-way mirror. The next week when Nicholas arrived, I told him I would be his tutor for this one session and asked him to tell me about himself. He said, "My name is Nicholas and I am 12 years old…. When I was six, they told me that I have dyslexia and would never learn to read and I have not ever learned…. I not only cannot read, I get an F in handwriting and math." He couldn't understand it, because he liked math. He was good at it, he could solve all the problems with mental calculations, and he could respond to questions orally. However, the teacher insisted on written responses on timed tests. This approach made Nick nervous; under pressure, he made may errors. Because of his poor grades, his father would not let him play with his friends after school. Instead, he was ordered to stay in his room and do homework. Nicholas was a very depressed 12-year-old as he stated, "I hate my life. I wish I was dead!"

Amazingly, Nicholas had diagnosed his problem. He was not learning to read because he believed he could not. He was bright, and could respond orally, but he had trouble with handwriting and became tense under pressure. My first step was to work on his attitude, which he had held for six years. First, I told him about Albert Einstein, Nelson Rockefeller, and Tom Cruise, to name a few dyslexic celebrities. Nicholas was very surprised to hear about them; he certainly did not think those men were dumb. I reassured him that he was not dumb, either, but he had not been given opportunities to learn. Nicholas was just like Patrick in Denny Taylor's *Learning Denied* (1991): The school system had failed him.

As we continued to work together, I asked Nicholas if he had ever used a computer. He had not. I introduced Nicholas to the talking computer with KidTalk software (Casey and Cron 1983). He immediately began to compose his life story. Then he read it and printed it out. "You are a very bright boy, Nicholas. You just needed a more sophisticated writing tool to help you put all your great ideas down on paper," I told him. Of course, it took more than a talking computer to help Nicholas; it took a teacher who understood his particular learning strengths and needs and who cared enough to encourage him and help him learn in other ways.

With the assistance of the computer, Nick's school work dramatically improved. (Better grades allowed him a better social life after school as well!) Nick was lucky—many students are not so lucky.

David Who Loved to Move and Discover

David was a first-grader I met when I was observing the use of networked computers in his K–1 classroom. I was reading a 10-page student story from the bulletin board when I heard a young boy's voice. "That's my story. Would you like me to read it to you?" "It's great," I said, "yes I would." He stood on a stool and started to read "The Life of Gorg Wasinton" (his inventive spelling). When he reached the tenth page, he said, "There's more in the computer. Do you want to hear some more?" "Absolutely!" I replied. He took me to one of the networked computers in the classroom, put head-phones on my head, located his file on the IBM network, and had his 26-page story read to me by the Primary Editor software. (For an excerpt, see figure 2.1.) As I read his writing, David watched me like a proud father. "Did you like it," he asked. "It was won-derful!" I replied. "May I have a copy to show teachers who think first-graders can only write a couple of sentences?" "Sure," he smiled.

After I read his story, I could hardly wait to speak with David's teacher. I said, "David must be a gifted first-grader. His story is outstanding, well above what you would expect from an average first-grader." She laughed, "Oh no," she said. "You should have seen him at the beginning of the year. He was identified ADD. He couldn't hold a pencil, and he hated school. Now he doesn't want to go out, even for recess, when he is in the middle of one of his great stories!"

9-18 dinusors lift 200 yers a goe They had fites. Evey day they had fites. One day a dinusor was eating gras. And a dinosaur got in a fites. The bigis dinnsor wan. it was nite time. it was snowing for a week.the dinsaurs dide. din pirit livd thay seld on the pirit ship. One day thay had a wor and the pirit wan the wor. Yers wint past it was 13-13. the pirate seld to america they had lots of wors. we had lots a people. So we got in the wor. it was a hornd. becaes they had canins. Some people tide it was sad. We won. We cunnit don it with the people who dide.thin gorchwoshtin live he was the first presit. He was born in ' 16-48.He was 1 yers old. He was nise he noow lots of thing. he had fan win he was 2 yers old he had tlooes. Noul he is 3 yers old he was omoste in pescol. noul he is 5 yers old he is in cinagarn.noul he is 6 yers]old he is in fiest gard. noul he is 7 yers old noul he is in secint gard.he finish secint gard.noulhe is 8 yers old.he is in 3 gard noul he is 9 yers old. yers wint pas. one day gorch woshintin did. it was sad we was criing.But we are stil a livi ornwe! sull we was still big noull. my gomo is a li8fe noull.and my gomo name is paling and she is 1 yers old. and she sleep in a cadle in her moms room and dads room it was nite time and poling was in moms and dads room sleeping in the cradl. the net day it was polings brthday and noull poling is 1 yers old and we had fon at the brthday to. it was nite time and poling had to sleep with mom and dad room she was sleeping in the cradle.in moms and dads room. days yint pis and it was polings brthday and she is was 2 yers old she had tlooes lick chats and lost a thing. and one day pling was biger and biger so we it was plings brthday and pling was 3 yers old and she had an remot control car and it was nite time and pling was sleeping in her own room and the net day plings mom both pling a puppy. Abraham lincoln was born on a farm in the state of Ken-tucky, and he,s birthday was February 12,1809.Abraham Lincoln was shot in the back.Abraham Lincoln had lots of friends and people hoo liked him.He and he was in a war and he won the war.He wint to go sots of plasis to go to study a bout the whole world.

Figure 2.1 David's story

I drove home thinking about a technology that had made a student write in a gifted manner even though he had been labeled a poor writer. This technology compelled a student who had been labeled with attention deficit disorder to sit for long periods of time thinking, creating, and imagining a 26-page story. If he could sit that long to write something of interest to him, then sitting still was not the problem; not having something worthwhile to attend to seemed a more likely problem. "Something is wrong with the labels," I concluded. "Students are fine when given the right tools and environment."

Thomas Armstrong, psychologist, teacher, and consultant, has years of experience working with children who have attention and behavior problems. He believes these children are, at core, fully intact, whole, and healthy human beings and that the best way to help them is to provide the kinds of nurturing, stimulating, and encouraging inventions that are good for all kids (Armstrong 1995). The computer provides nurturing, stimulation, and control in the learning environment. All teachers need to provide is encouragement.

Quote

Writing Process with Speech Enhancement

Speech-enhanced word processing programs allow beginning English learners to hear any word. They allow proficient language users to play with speed, pitch, volume, and sound. Thus speech capability has something to offer all language learners. It also is an excellent tool for revising text.

Codey, Nicholas, and David—along with about 1,000 other 5–12 year olds I have worked with—have convinced me of the importance of having talking computers available to students in every classroom. The computer should not be used as only a reward for completing assignments or as a drill-and-kill machine. Rather, it should be used as a tool to think with, a sophisticated pencil, a tool to solve problems and to record a person's own language experience. The computer allows the young child the ability to create letters, words and stories long before their own small muscle coordination allows them to create clear DeNealian letters using the old tool, the pencil.

In *Living Between the Lines*, Lucy Calkins (1991) gives exciting ideas for writer's workshops and how to get children to write. This book has outstanding information on the writing process, but it hardly mentions those who cannot translate their creative thoughts and oral language into pencil marks on paper. These children need a tool that allows them to tell their stories, a tool that empowers their emergent literacy, that convinces them they are literate and intelligent. In the meantime, they can do lots of drawing and other activities that gives their small muscle coordination time to develop and soon they will write successfully in each medium.

With this new technology, the writing process differs from what has been practiced in classrooms. It is not necessary—in fact, it is detrimental—for students to write their stories first in pencil and then to type them. This process negates the power of the word processor to give easier access to print and quick, easy editing. Students can think as they type and write their story as they imagine it. The teacher's role is as interested listener and coach. By having the students read their writing to you, you can provide appropriate feedback to help them expand and develop their writings. Inventive spelling should be accepted as the first, rough-draft stage of beginning writers. The emphasis should be content and flow of thought before editing is attempted. The talking word processor is very helpful in the editing process. As students hear their own story read back to them by the computer they often become aware of changes they need or want to make.

Most of all, the computer empowers students by allowing them to instantly produce professional-looking print. For the first time, they have the experience of producing a readable story and realizing they can be an author and not a member of the low-reading group.

This new tool can bring success to many students who have previously fallen through educational cracks.

No More Labels

Labels have disastrous effects on children. In the previous examples, each boy was labeled: Low, low group for Codey; dyslexic for Nicholas; ADD for David. In each case, the label fostered the student's belief he could not be successful—and he was not.

During a visit to Maungawhau School in Auckland, New Zealand, I witnessed the excitement of students in the whole-language classrooms who were creating drawings, writing stories, and publishing. Everyone was excited and included. No students were standing alone in the hall as punishment, no names were on the board. When I spoke to the school director, she had one observation to share. "I believe we have much greater success with our whole language programs ... because we do not label our children as you do in the States. We treat them as if they all can learn. As you have seen today, they do!"

Lessons learned from students in the United States and around the world teach us to include all children in integrated listening, speaking, writing, and reading classrooms and teach us that the speech-enhanced computer can be a valued tool in every classroom to assist all students in achieving literacy success. This important use of the computer should be for language processing. This is the process of students, by themselves, putting down their own thoughts and feelings (language-experience stories) using a talking word processor and then receiving the auditory reinforcement of hearing their own words spoken back to them.

In *Using Computers in the Teaching of Reading*, the authors found that, in classrooms in which teachers replace pencil and paper with computers, children write more, revise more willingly and more extensively, and work longer on a single piece. The result is not only longer, more detailed, and generally better pieces of writing, but realization by the children that they can manipulate text, changing it at will and as often as they like to produce the effect they want (Strickland 1987).

How Language Processing Fits into a Literature-Based Reading Program

Writing competence, it is hypothesized, comes only from large amounts of self-motivated reading for interest and pleasure. It is acquired subconsciously; readers are unaware they are acquiring writing competence while they are reading (Krashen

1984). In a literature-based program, teachers read daily to students, and students also read self-selected books for interest and pleasure. All the ingredients exist to produce excellent writers. But in the case of students whose visual–motor skills do not allow them to express ideas on paper with pencil, the talking computer can be the means to achieve the success their peers have already experienced. The student who in the past experienced early failure and developed a negative attitude toward learning can now find success. In fact, this student often does so well at the word processor that he can help others in the class master it, with the resultant boost to his self-esteem that has been so sorely missing.

Summary

The language machine has grown and evolved rapidly since its birth in the 1980s. The synthesized speech is much more natural and it speaks in several languages. Its potential as a tool to empower young children in their journey to literacy has been shown to be effective around the world. The one caution is that it must be used to empower children's own written language development, not as an electronic work-book. Our goal now is to offer every child this unique learning tool and to help teachers understand the power of this tool to create the best possible learning environment for all students.

Chapter 3

The Discovery of Written Language in the Computer Age

Rachel Cohen, Ph.D.
University Paris–Nord

I have always been fascinated by the remarkable potential of young children. This is why I decided to start my professional career as a kindergarten teacher, although I had a degree in philosophy that entitled me to teach older students. But observing young children ages three to six daily seemed to me the best way to know them better. I soon realized that the more I offered them, the more they wanted and the more they enjoyed it. Teaching in a bilingual school, I taught English as well as French. The children enjoyed singing and, speaking English, which was a foreign language to them, switching easily from one language to another. In French, I had the habit of writing their names, the new words we learned, our stories. At the end of the year, to my amazement, I realized the children could read (Cohen 1977).

A great controversy ensued; many educators and psychologists defended the idea that young children, before age six, could not and should not learn how to read! But I was persuaded to the contrary. I interviewed renowned specialists, biologists, neurophysiologists, linguists, educators from around the world, all of whom agree young children have great potential and can achieve much more than what we generally expect of them, provided they are given the opportunity to use it (Cohen 1982). I also showed in a longitudinal study that children who were exposed to early reading and bilingualism in a very stimulating environment developed mental abilities that children in control groups did not develop at the same age (Cohen et al 1989). Furthermore, I realized this educational approach is the best way to prevent school failure and illiteracy, particularly among children living in very poor areas whose mother tongue is not French. My next research in a school located in a northern suburb of Paris, supported this belief (Cohen 1988).

One problem remained: Although the children were able to read, they were unable to write their stories in a readable manner because of insufficient motor coordination (which did not mean that they were unable to express themselves in a written form). At that time, around the 1980s, computers were starting to be introduced into universities and secondary schools. I realized then that there lay the answer. What if we also used computers with very young children? Many issues remained to be resolved: Could young children use

computers? Could they use computers for learning purposes? Did we have adequate soft-
ware? How would very young children react to this new tool? Would it affect their learning
processes? Their ability to learn? Their achievement? New research was required to answer
these fundamental questions.

Early Attempts to Use Computers with Young Children

When computers started invading school systems all over the world, only 15
years ago, priority was given to senior classes, then primary classes. Seldom did one
see computers in kindergartens or preprimary schools. Was the new tool considered a
threat to the mental or social growth of young children? Or were young children considered incapable of using it?

In homes, it was the same story: Parents would first buy a computer for themselves, but would soon realize their children were better at using it than they were.
When little ones came around the computer, trying to put their fingers on the keyboard, they were chased away by their older brothers or sisters who insisted this toy
was not for them.

The controversy among adults raged: Some educators or parents felt that the magic
aspect of this new tool would give children a wrong picture of real learning or would
keep them away from fundamental activities necessary for child growth; others were
afraid that children would be isolated in an individual learning situation, that would be
harmful to social growth; others were afraid that the linear aspect of programmed
instruction would kill creativity or cognitive development. On the other hand, many
others felt these new ways of learning would develop in children new ways of thinking
(new processes of learning, as Papert would say [Papert 1980]), allowing them to
manipulate symbols at an early age, thus enhancing mental development (Hess 1986).

For this last category of adults, the computer was not a simple new pedagogical
tool to teach old things in a new way, but a tool capable of opening new horizons in
education, of developing new mental processes, new behaviors (Lawler 1985). But in
this case, it was essential to create around children a stimulating environment capable
of developing in them an attitude of exploration and discovery.

In schools, the first attempts offered the child were mainly games using the light
pen or the joy stick. Then came the games enhancing concepts that were considered
important in their development: space, numbers, letters, prereading activities. In June
1986, at an international conference on reading in London, we heard about an experiment with young children using only a few keys in reading-readiness activities. It was
considered a revolution!

A huge number of changes have occurred since the 1980s. It is not my purpose to
review the important developments that have taken place. Instead, I would like to focus
on the various research projects I have led over the last 15 years, and investigate the
psychological and educational issues of a computerized environment for young children and the new learning conditions offered by computers for the discovery of the
written language.

Can Technology Improve the Learning Abilities of Young Children?

The object of the first research (1983–1986) was to (1) investigate ways of using the computer in the learning process, particularly in the learning of written language by very young children, and (2) to develop the use of the computer as an educational tool by studying its effects on the organization of time and space in the learning environment, on children's behavior, and on their interpersonal relationships (Cohen et al 1987). At that time, using this new tool raised important educational issues: How can a stimulating situation help a child's learning process, particularly in the discovery of the written language? Are very young children able to use a computer? A keyboard? How can a computer center be integrated in all activities of a preschool class? How can children become independent and autonomous in a computer center? How can a program enhance a child's creativity and activity, but respect personality?

About 600 children, age three to ten, from all parts of France, representing all socioeconomic backgrounds, took part in the experiment. Among them were non-French speaking children and children with learning difficulties, as well as emotionally disturbed children. The research was carried out by the Learning Group of the Centre Mondial Informatique et Resource Humaine in Paris.

Preliminary Questions

Before summarizing the research findings, three fundamental preliminary questions must be answered: Why the focus on very young children? Why the written language? Why use the computer when other means of instruction are available?

Why Focus on Young Children?

The research is based on the assumption that very young children have immense potential. Their learning capabilities are far greater than they appear under usual classroom conditions. Bloom (Bloom 1964), states that "exceptional levels of talent development require certain types of environmental support, special experience, excellent teaching and appropriate motivational encouragement at each stage of development." The geneticist Jacquard says, "every child is a potential superman" and adds, "What I am, I am by virtue of heritage; what I become depends on what I do with it." Children will be able to develop their inner potential only in an environment that is rich and full of stimulation of all kinds. In order that the neurobiological system may function, there must be an activity, there must be optimal stimulation (Cohen 1982). Indeed, if the neurobiological circuits are not exercised very early in life, they may never function at their peak. Therefore, during the first years of life, it is necessary to recognize the cognitive needs of young children, their wish and potential to learn. The question then becomes: Under what conditions is the computer a stimulative tool in the child's environment?

Why Focus on Written Language?

The conclusions of previous research conducted with several educational teams in France in various socioeconomic environments, and in particular in underprivileged and non-French–speaking communities, among various age groups and mother tongues, coincide with the results found in other countries: Before age six, young children want to learn to read, can learn to read, and take pleasure in learning to read, so long as the methodology respects the learning processes specific to this age group (Cohen 1977; Cohen 1982; Cohen et al 1987). The question is: Under what conditions can the computer aid the discovery of written language for young children?

Why the Computer?

This key question encompasses many important issues. Is a young child, from age three to six, able to use a computer, not only for playing but also for learning? What situations are likely to enhance creative and autonomous learning? Under what conditions can the computer be introduced and integrated in all the activities of a kindergarten classroom?

The first investigations focused on the question: Is the young child able to use a computer? The answers were massively: Yes. Even the child who does not read can use a keyboard. Observations of children using a light pen or keyboard clearly indicated that, even before age three, children want and are able to use a computer.

With this premise, the focus changes. The questions become: What can children learn? Under what conditions?

All of the learning processes described by Piaget—interactivity, personal activity of the child who can observe the effects of actions and adjust them progressively, positive reinforcement and feedback, exploratory activity—should be present in appropriate software.

Such a learning situation certainly gives children interesting opportunities for self-correction, multiple experiences, and the ability to work at their own pace in an independent learning situation. It also provides opportunity for exchanges, cooperation, group learning, and social interaction with playmates who can share and help each other. The laughs and constant exchanges in the computer center prove such learning is a happy experience for the children. Though one child may be on the keyboard, all the children around the computer benefit from the activity. Thus, if software is carefully designed and respects the psychological development of children, the computer can offer particularly fruitful conditions that enhance creative and autonomous or shared learning.

The Role of the Computer

What is the role of the computer in the discovery and exploration of the written language?

In order to learn how to read, a child is generally placed in front of a page full of written signs. When the computer is used, the child may be placed in front of a blank screen to fill. Under these circumstances, the double function of the written language emerges: The child both sends and receives messages. This is why the term *written language* is preferred to the word *reading*. *Written language* highlights the idea that using written language is a communication process.

The computer offers the young child special opportunities for important discoveries. First is the discovery of the direction and spatial structure of the written language, which is revealed as the screen is filled from left to right. Second, the use of the space bar allows the child to feel what a word is. The same is true of letters: Again, by tactical feeling, the child discovers the placement of letters. Very young children using computers do not confuse words with letters; in other learning situations *word* and *letter* are abstract terms. Even the productions of very young children are readable. This supports the idea that written language is a means of expression and communication usable by very young children.

In addition to discoveries, the computer offers a special level of satisfaction to young users. In this, the delete key plays an important role. No mistakes remain in the eyes of the children, and they enjoy their neat productions. For young, clumsy children, this is a real, rewarding pleasure. In short, the written language is, from the very beginning, a communication tool, and children are not prisoners of their motor skills and capabilities. This means of communication is dual, right from the beginning, allowing reading as well as writing.

The Research: Experimental and Evaluation Procedures

The research started in September 1983 and ended in June 1986. The multidisciplinary research team included educators, psychologists, computer scientists, and programmers.

Not only was the team able to observe individually the ability of very young children to use a computer, it confirmed the hypothesis that very young children, before age six, are able to discover and learn written language using this new educational device. At that time, no appropriate software existed. Therefore the team created software, tested it, remodeled it after observation of the children and evaluation, and extended the experiment to large populations (Programmes ALE). The research was not linear, for each stage of the work allowed not only remodeling of the software but produced new ideas for new pieces of software.

The first year of the research (1983–1984) was devoted essentially to two tasks. This first task was creation of tools, which included design and production of software, as well as tools for observation and data collection. The second task was experimentation in four classrooms involving about 150 children (Barriere and Plaisant 1986). The object was to observe children as they used the software and to evaluate and modify the software in the light of the observation. Another purpose was to develop new software. Finally, we wanted to clarify the relationship between spontaneous play and structured learning, and we wanted to identify areas of high motivation.

The evaluation included observation of the children, both direct and in videos of them; construction of an observation grid for describing child behavior; regular interviews with teachers; and development and analysis of stored data.

During the second year (1984–1985), the project was extended to Paris, Parisian suburbs, Marseille, day care centers, and rural schools. Six hundred children, three to eight, of various socioeconomic backgrounds and mother tongues, took part in the research (Naymark and Plaisant 1986). This extension made it necessary to review and improve data collection by use of a log in which the teachers recorded their observations every week; case studies; analysis of children's work; development of a database that allowed data collection and processing.

During the third year (1985–1986), the research was extended to specific school populations: the follow-up of kindergarten children now in first grade; children with great learning difficulties, particularly reading disabilities; and non–French–speaking children in immigrant environment. The same type of evaluation took place as in the first phase, that is, observation, both direct and via video, and regular interviews with teachers.

The A.L.E. (*Apprentissage Langue Ecrite*) Software

The best way to describe the process of the software designed is to compare it with the way a child acquires oral language in meaningful situations: Learning as opposed to teaching. The child is never asked to acquire a specific skill and is not constrained by any definite progression. Children build knowledge through experiences, at their own pace. They are the master of their own actions; they will explore. In a word they *learn* in the Piagetian sense of the word, in situations that call for imagination and creativity. The written language is not an end in itself, but a tool with which to undertake other tasks, such as creating a picture with predetermined objects that the child calls to the screen by means of the light pen, mouse, or keyboard. The learning situation combines play and imitation, which are two important factors in a learning process.

In the first part of the program, the aim of the child is to produce a lovely picture by choosing predefined objects. Topics from which to choose are: landscape, zoo, beach, farm, town, blocks, and shapes. In each topic there are 20 words. The child may call these objects on the screen by pointing to the word with the light pen, by clicking on it with the mouse, or by typing it on the keyboard. (Typing involves copying the word from a picture book, even though the child might not know the names of the letters being typed.) The program offers a double approach to the written language: A *global* approach, when the child uses the light pen or the mouse to click on a specific word, and an *analytical* approach, when the child types the word letter by letter. In both approaches, the shape of words and their meaning are clear to the child because the picture appears on the screen. The child then moves the object by means of the arrows, thus producing a lovely picture on the screen. The combinations are endless: The pictures on the screen enhance the child's imagination and far exceed the child's drawing skills, thus encouraging the aesthetic aspect in pictorial compositions. The pictures obtained would never be within the child's reach otherwise. In the second part of the program, the child can write the story of the picture or any other story using an easy word processor provided in the program.

In the second-generation programs, the library of pictures included 80 pictures, and voice synthesis was incorporated. Furthermore, each child in the class had 10 pages in a file. This allowed each child to write long stories or continue a story the next day, to go back to a previous page or choose to work on a new story, to send a copy of the work to a friend, and to change the size or type of font. Thus the children used and understood computer commands.

Findings

In this new educational context, one can wonder whether old pedagogical models should not be redefined. It is impossible to list all the interesting observations made during these long and fruitful years. This section points out some interesting features.

Child Behavior

The joy and enthusiasm observed in these children leads us to think that computers may be a very good thing for young children and that written language can be acquired just as easily as oral language, without tedious repetitions or predefined progression.

The increasing motivation for writing and reading transfers to other activities, even for children with great learning difficulties. There is increasing interest in the language itself, and very young children may become interested in sentence structure, spelling, and punctuation.

Finally, the power of attention and concentration is simply amazing, and contradicts what is generally known about the abilities of young children to concentrate for long periods of time. We were compelled to send children to other activities after 30 minutes. They refused to play outdoors and sometimes hid in the classroom instead of going to lunch!

One may wonder what is the frontier between play and work? How can one explain such behaviors? Is it the magic aspect of the machine? New learning conditions? The software itself? All these factors have a role to play, but mainly what this learning tool really provides is a response to the child's deep need to learning and to develop personal strategies and creativity.

Children and Computers

There is no doubt that very young children, even age three, are able to use a computer and the entire keyboard with great interest and pleasure. The computer fascinates small children and serves as a valuable learning tool. In addition, it helps children in areas considered beyond their capabilities, if all conditions needed to enhance learning are provided in a good piece of software. Thus, good software design is essential, as is teacher training. Some teachers think computers will replace them; others think the computer is only one new pedagogical tool among others. Neither of these opinions are true: Computers open fascinating horizons that go far beyond educational aims.

Discovery of Written Language

Under these new pedagogical conditions, can or should we analyze the reading processes as we did before?

Children have shown they are experts in oral language. Now they are showing us they can be experts in its visual aspect. In this approach, we are dealing with learning processes and not teaching methods. Thus, the line between global and analytical methods of reading become blurred to the point it is no longer appropriate to speak of them as separate, distinct methods. Children switch from one approach to the other according to their needs. They are not only capable of recognizing or writing letters, but they are able to use words, whole sentences, and stories. The fact that their work is always neat and that they can print it for their parents or playmates, that they may keep it or send it to grandma, gives them the scope of what written language can do for them. Thus, using written language becomes a quite exciting experience!

We can no longer speak of the prerequisites necessary to start reading, nor can we accept the assertion that a child younger than age six cannot, or should not, learn to read. Nor can we accept the analysis of how a child discovers what the written language is (Ferreiro 1986). Children will master the written language as they have mastered the oral language—by using it.

Written language is perceived in its real function as a new means of communication. It does not require speaking aloud to be understood. It has meaning, and it can be understood by others. The child finds in written language a new means of expression, although motor coordination is not mature enough to "write." Why should written language be linked to the physical development of the child? Why should we accept the rule that "the acquisition of written language supposes first the possibility of controlling and guiding movement to be able to reproduce a model" (Lurçat 1985).

What we considered difficult for young children is now within their reach. Spelling is acquired as they type. No specific learning or progression is needed. First they type one letter at a time, then a few together, then whole words, without even looking at the model. Such was the case of a four-year-old boy who wanted a sky studded with stars. When he typed the word *star* for the thirty-sixth time, he certainly did not need the model! (And *star*, in French, is a difficult word: *étoile*.)

It is beyond the scope of this article to describe how a child masters graphemes and phonemes and succeeds in writing the new words that are necessary to stories. By analyzing similarities and differences, in a dynamic, repeated use of known words, where mistakes are self-corrected, the child discovers the rules of spelling as well as the rules of sentence construction.

There is no problem with punctuation, use of capital letters, or paragraphs—all features that have been left to eight or nine year olds and would not have been expected of kindergartners. Observation shows that the more expert children become, the more they want to write and the longer their stories become. Moreover, their interest in stories and books increases in an amazing way. Cooperative work and exchanges play a most important role in these activities.

The experiment carried out with older children, age seven to nine, also showed that children have never written so much before. The computer helps, in a significant way, children who have reading and writing problems, children with severe learning disabilities, emotionally disturbed children, and non-French–speaking immigrant children. In these groups, the results went far beyond the hopes of educators and researchers.

In short, the findings of this research require us to dismiss the old, meaningless debate about different methodological approaches of what is reading and accept the fact that all children, even very young ones, are fascinated by language, oral or written. The computer not only stimulates them in a new environment, it gives them new learning powers and new paths to thought. This is what we want to give to all children!

Computers and the Acquisition of a Foreign Language

The second research (Cohen 1988) was concerned with children who encounter great difficulties in their school life and who, as a result, become school failures. These include children who do not learn to read in primary school, children with great psychological and behavioral problems, deaf children, and children belonging to immigrant families who do not speak French at home. We shall concentrate on this last category.

Bilingualism, or learning a foreign language, is no longer a problem we should look upon as we did only a few years ago. It is not a question of whether children should learn a foreign language at an early age. Bilingualism is a fact: The frontiers have opened and the world has shrunk because of advanced means of transportation, and media, fostering international exchanges. Moreover, most countries face a bilingual situation within their own frontiers.

So, the question is a how-to question. What methodologies can best help children to learn a foreign language? What role can the new technologies play in this urgent integration process?

In Europe, we can no longer speak of immigrant children, but rather of a pluricultural and a multilingual community. Ours is a diversified population. European children have to know at least two or three languages. In certain districts of large European towns, the problem of integrating children of different nationalities, cultures, and languages is crucial. It has been proven that it is among this group of children, many of whose parents do not speak French and who, in certain cases, are illiterate in their own language, that the greatest number fail in the first activity they have to undertake in their school life: Learning to read.

When we started working in this field, the official statistics for 1981 were alarming: 16% of the children failed in the first year of primary school. This shows that a large proportion of the children start on their school career with a definite handicap that will increase during the following years. The percentage of underachievers at the end of their fifth year in primary school was:

Pupils one year behind schedule	30%
Pupils two years behind schedule	15%
Pupils three years or more behind schedule	3%

These figures testify to the great difficulties pupils encounter in learning basic subjects when reading is not achieved during the first year. The school where this research was carried out holds one of the saddest records for failure: The total number of failures was 61.5%, which was 23.5% more than the national average.

Among the pupils encountering difficulties, a higher proportion come from families of an unfavorable socioeconomic environment; more especially, these children are not French-speaking or have attended preschool for only a short period of time. In the district where this research was undertaken, the population consisted almost entirely of working-class families. Most of the fathers were manual workers (72%); most of the mothers had no occupation (56%). With regard to nationalities during the years of the research project, an important development was noticed:

Academic Year	Number of Foreign Children
1980	52%
1983	63%
1987	more than 75%

Today, the percentage of foreign children in this district is as high as 90%.

These figures highlight the fact that the problem is not a pedagogical one; it is a human and social problem, for it is a matter of fighting academic failure and failure in life.

To work in such conditions was a real challenge. Is the computer a tool which could be of assistance in this situation to prevent illiteracy and school failure?

The Issues

The problem that concerned us directly was to find out whether the computer could make a major contribution to the teaching of French as a foreign language to children three to six years old (Cohen 1992a). We raised questions which, in so-called classical education, have been solved quite differently. In so doing, we upset many firmly rooted beliefs. Can young children learn a foreign language in their early years without suffering harmful effects? If this question is answered in the affirmative, it is generally accepted that young children must first learn a foreign language orally before learning to write it.

The second question is to discover whether young children are able to come to grips with learning a foreign language orally and in writing. Under what conditions can they do so? What are the practical methods to be used? What happens to the learning of the mother tongue or any other means of communication within the family?

Research to answer these questions was built on the basis of certain conclusions from our previous work: First, children under the age of six are able to use a computer, not only as a play tool but also as a learning tool. Second, children can, with the help of appropriate software suited to their capabilities, curiosity, needs, and interests, discover the written language; they do so with pleasure, with ease, and by interacting with companions, if these programs are geared to the process of discovery and learning inherent in young children.

The Research

The class in which the research was carried out over five years included foreign children age three to six from various countries. It was not a ghetto classroom, for its flexible structure allowed for the integration of these children into other classes to participate in other activities. The common denominator is that these children did not speak a word of French at the beginning of the academic year or when they were admitted to the school. The research project was original in two ways: First, it aimed to teach French as a second language by means of a computer. Second, it aimed at simultaneously developing both the oral and written French language. (Many would describe this approach as heresy.)

The software used is described on page 32. Voice synthesis was added in the second year of this project.

Writing to Read, Reading to Speak

The order generally used in the teaching of a foreign language is speaking, reading, and writing. But in fact, in our situation, these functions are reversed: The child, writing a word, makes the picture appear; the picture, in turn gives a clue to the meaning of the word. For the non-French–speaking child this is even more important than for other children. Contrary to the usual situations, it is the written word that comes first. Before the use of the voice synthesizer, the teacher had to pronounce the word in order to help the child read it. Now, with the voice synthesizer, the situation is changed: The child is able to read what is written and to pronounce all the words.

The picture is the starting point to remarks, comments, and dialogues based on the child's own experience. As many children are always gathering around the computer, exchanges and discussions create a climate of very lively interactions and communications, even though the children may be of different mother tongues. The French language becomes the lingua franca. Once the picture is finished, the adult helps the child slide more precisely into the oral vocabulary ("the oral image of the word") to establish links between the various parts of the drawing by forming sentences and by generally making up a story. In this last activity, the idea is the child's, but the teacher helps to correct sentences and to enlarge grammatical structures as well as vocabulary. The teacher then writes the story on a slip of paper that the child types into the computer, then prints.

Having created his or her own text, the child, by an interesting logical process, will be able to read it or guess at most of what is written. Thus, there is constant, two-way dynamic between the oral and the written language. In this way, books are created by the children and become part of the class library with free access to everyone.

A New Approach to Written Language in Foreign Language Learning

The computer has developed a new approach to the learning of a foreign language by young children. Indeed, what is written can be said, and what is said can be written. The points of reference are to be found at the hearing level but also at the visual level, which is much more permanent and can be referred to at any time. Learning is thus made easier. One can go so far as to say that understanding a language with the eye is easier for the young child than understanding it with the ear.

Increasing one's vocabulary becomes an attractive game for the non-French–speaking child. When a word is mispronounced, the teacher can make use of the written word and in particular, use the words of the program, to correct the child. Indeed, the child is sensitive to the written signs and often refers to them. By the end of the year, many children try to write new words by listening, looking, and comparing with what they already know; they are also keen on writing stories. Precious time has been gained in oral as well as in written work, especially by those children who are going to be admitted to the first year of primary school in the following academic year.

What has been said does not refer only to very young children, as this research has shown; nor does it refer to the French language in particular. New technologies must prompt new educational strategies and new thinking in the teaching of foreign languages.

Stories Have to Speak

This sentence, repeated by a teacher over and over again, led us to add a new feature to the research. Conscious of the importance of the listening process and oral immersion, we tried a new device that would enable the children to listen to their own stories constantly and whenever they felt like it. We set up the sound library. The children's own stories were recorded on a tape with their own drawings, which made the meaning clear. Each child's stories were recorded, and all the stories were freely accessible to the children. The children could listen to the stories at any moment of the day, while looking at the book (the printout of the story). Both the author and the other children in the class loved it.

In spite of this device, a link was missing in the simultaneous discovery process of both oral and written language. Two problems had to be solved: First, though the children, by the end of the year, had a pretty good idea of the alphabet, their discoveries were made at random and we were not able, nor did we want to help them systematically. Second, the children were not able by themselves to pronounce new words that they produced by writing them on the computer; though they understood the meaning by looking at the pictures, they needed the teacher's help to pronounce them correctly.

This led us to explore the possibilities of voice synthesis.

Conclusions

This research, so rich in many ways, is a challenge to accepted theories. It compels us to question our own beliefs. New technologies open new outlooks, and old methodologies no longer apply.

Young children who do not speak the language spoken in class show that they are capable of much more than we thought possible. Not only do they develop new skills, they also develop an ability to concentrate that is unusual at that age. They show they can be independent and self-reliant in areas of learning where, hitherto, the teacher ruled. Finally, they show that learning behaviors induced by the computer can be transferred to other fields of activities.

More than a mere tool, the computer has changed the organization of the classroom, giving to the teacher a new and more gratifying role to play. Tedious tasks, such as repetition, correction, and organization of the learning process, are taken over by the children themselves.

The process of teaching and learning a foreign language needs to be reviewed with respect to most favorable starting age, methods, role of written language, and simultaneous learning of oral as well as written language.

Last, but most important, this research shows that children of various mother tongues and children of low socioeconomic backgrounds should not, by any means, be considered candidates for failure in school!

When the Computer Speaks: Use of the Voice Synthesizer

This third research (1989–1992) addresses the question whether the use of a computer equipped with a voice synthesizer will make a major contribution to the learning process. In what ways will the use of a voice synthesizer affect the results already obtained?

Rapid word decoding and phonological awareness seem essential to the process of learning to read. Thus, the questions are: What is the effect of speech output, as a tool, in such specific areas, such as reading and foreign language learning (Cohen 1992a; Cohen 1992b)? Is auditory feedback an essential part of the learning process in general?

The school population we had been working with came from various social environments, but this report concentrates on nonfrancophone children age three to six attending preschool in a suburb located north of Paris.

Again, the challenge was great: The discovery of the French language as a foreign language, both written and oral, to nonfrancophone children below the age of six, with the support of a computer equipped with a voice synthesizer was indeed an exceptional educational situation that upset firmly rooted beliefs. In this research the focus was on the effect of the new variable: voice input.

The Research

During this research, the computer was installed in the classroom in a self-service situation. The computer center was a place where interactions are rich and numerous. The computer that speaks was at first, an object of curiosity and of questioning. The child was led to discover its possibilities by trial and error, this time with the help of voice feedback. Very soon, the enthusiasm engendered was so great that access to the computer had to be regulated.

In this stage of the research, the voice output allowed the child to hear every letter as it was typed, every word as it was completed by pressing the space bar, and the whole text when the story was finished. Though children were free to ask the computer not to speak, it very quickly became clear that children asked the computer to speak and felt frustrated if it did not! From the start, the voice synthesizer appeared to be an enjoyable game that gave much satisfaction to the children. The teacher no longer had to worry about repetition: The children spontaneously repeated the letters or words the computer spoke. Even children who were not typing, and those who were busy in another part of the classroom, echoed the computer's speech. Thus, the link was made between the oral and visual image of words.

Furthermore, voice synthesis acts as a tool for checking and self-correction when children write. If what they hear is not what they expect, they are able to correct their mistakes without the help of the teacher. The voice synthesizer also allowed children to explore the written language. Putting letters together and listening to what they produce is a game many children undertake before writing real words, just as babies play with sounds before uttering real words.

Another most important feature is the self-satisfaction children express when they are able to listen to their own stories and hear their own name as authors. Children listen to their own stories over and over again with obvious pleasure, calling other children to listen, too. Writing has meaning for them, and positive feedback is always present.

Findings

The problem for this research was not to evaluate in the traditional manner the performances of the experimental group compared with a control group: To discover whether these children perform better or not with such equipment. Rather, we were primarily concerned with observing what the children would do in this new learning situation and what would be their strategies to master this new tool. Our aim was to better understand the process of learning when sound produced by the child intervenes in the learning process and acquisition of language.

For all these reasons and to fit our purpose, we decided to employ qualitative evaluation based on regular observations, case studies, analysis of productions, and interviews of the teachers. This is consistent with what we did with the previous research.

A New Playmate: The Voice

With voice synthesis, the computer became personalized, it became part of the game. It was spoken to or scolded if it did not react the way the children wished! The starting point for motivation, which is an important factor in the acquisition of language, is dialogue based on the child's own experience. That dialogue, and the child's state of knowledge, is enhanced by the voice synthesizer.

For the non-French speaking children, the image that appears on the screen as they write clarifies the meaning of the written word. The voice synthesizer allows the child to also listen to the word just written and to pronounce it correctly. In contrast to the usual educational situations, the written word comes before the spoken word. The fact that the letters are pronounced as they are typed makes the children aware of how the word is constructed; thus, spelling becomes a game. The children repeat the letters as they appear on the screen. We even observed children at play pronouncing the letter before the computer! When the word is pronounced, the child is able to link the written word, its meaning (by the picture produced), and its pronunciation.

After the picture is finished, the adult helps the child tell his or her own story, enlarge the vocabulary, and correct the child's sentences. Finally, the child writes the story on the computer and prints it. Children love hearing their own stories over and over again, especially when they have signed the stories, so that the computer announces their name as author. This is a very rewarding situation. Written language becomes a means of self-expression.

Value of Voice Synthesis

Children who have written their own texts are able to read them (or guess most of what is written), whatever their age. There is a constant interchange between the oral and the written language. This interaction between all processes of communication is dynamic; each phase of the learning process interacts with all of the others, but the listening component is present at every level of the process.

In summarizing this aspect of the evaluation, we find again that we can no longer speak of reading or writing or spelling as independent activities, but rather must speak of the acquisition of language, in which no definite progression is followed by the teacher. The children use any word they need or know, however difficult it may be. Spelling is an activity within the reach of very young children, they acquire the words as they use them, and the teacher does not have to ask them to repeat.

The acquisition of knowledge goes far beyond what can be expected of young children. For example, when children write a text without punctuation, the voice synthesizer reads it without stops, and it makes no sense. When the children react to this reading, the teacher explains the need for punctuation and capitalization. Even children four or five years old are quite capable of mastering such notions.

In a traditional situation of learning, the teacher is the main source of information. But with the computer, the situation is completely different. The computer offers multiple sources of information and of self-correction. We have analyzed six ways of seeking and finding information, some of which are linked with the learning situation as a whole and not specifically to the computer:

the computer program, which is self-correcting;

the voice synthesizer, which allows the child to hear if a word is written incorrectly;

other children (let us not forget the computer is an excellent means of cooperative and group work);

other sources, such as books, dictionaries, word lists, and materials made by the children themselves; and, finally,

the adult, who is the ultimate resource when other means fail.

The Children's Behavior

Beyond the acquisition of knowledge, the construction of the children's personalities is more important than the actual result of a picture or a text produced. In fact, this learning situation encourages self-learning and self-organization; self-awareness develops and the effect of voice synthesizer is particularly important in this respect; self-esteem is encouraged: Children are proud of their results whatever they may be. No frustration is felt if a mistake occurs because the voice feedback acts as a positive reinforcement; the span of concentration and attention grows. We have observed children below five years of age staying more than 45 minutes at the computer, they have to be dragged away to go to recess or to go home. The children work at a greater speed and it seems that parallel auditory and visual feedback enhances the development of memory. At the end of the year we observed that children had developed their own method of work and that the previous acquisitions helped them to become more and more efficient. They also learned to share, to cooperate between themselves, the voice making the computer even more "sociable" than usual. But, to us, the most important observation of all was the pleasure of working, for example, the explosions of laughter and joy heard, especially when the computer said "silly things" (misspelled words that sound funny).

Conclusions

Children of all ages, whatever their nationalities, mother tongues, or knowledge of French, are encouraged in their learning processes by the new learning situation involving computers with synthesized speech. It seems clear that voice output enhances the awareness and the speed of acquisition of learning, particularly in the acquisition of written language and the learning of a foreign language.

Children who took part in the program and entered primary school at the age of six had a solid basic knowledge of the language, both oral and written, and their reading ability was far beyond any group of French children who had not had these opportunities. The problem we encountered was that of teachers following up these approaches later in primary school.

Theoretically, this research using voice output made us revise what we thought we knew about learning to read and the strategies of teaching and learning a foreign language.

What We Thought We Knew and What We Now Know

Learning theories, methods of teaching, and educational approaches have proliferated over the years. Various camps have defended their views with extensive research and comparative studies. Discussions have raged for decades. In recent years, a new dimension has been added. Psychologists and educators have began to face unexpected educational situations.

Only a few years ago it was believed:

- young children below age six could not and should not learn how to read; could not and should not learn a foreign language too early, or at least should master their mother tongue before being exposed to a foreign language; could not use computers or could use them only for play;
- learning to read was a silent process, going from eye to brain, a process acquired before writing because of the young child's poor motor coordination; and
- in the learning of a foreign language, young children should first master the language orally before learning to read and write it.

In what ways do the new technologies change the process of learning for young children? Using computers with young children under the age of six has changed a number of our beliefs.

The Key Questions

In the field of reading, the traditional questions are: What is the best starting age? What reading readiness exercises are required before starting to read? What are the prerequisites? The reading methods? Should children learn to speak before learning to read? Should they learn to read before learning to write? Is reading a silent process?

In the field of foreign-language learning, the main questions are: When should young children learn a foreign language? Should they master their mother tongue first, before starting a foreign language? Should they first learn to speak before learning to read and write?

In the field of computer use, new questions arise: Are young children, aged three to six, able to use a computer as a learning tool, in addition to enjoying it as a play tool? How can teachers integrate computer activities in the normal curriculum of a preschool? What are the effects of computer use on behavior, strategies of learning, and relationships?

What We Know About Learning to Read

There is no particular age to start acquiring the written language, and it is wrong to think that young children should acquire reading only when they have the proper motor coordination to write. Using computers shows that very young children are quite capable of using the keyboard to write and send readable, clear messages that other people can read. Not only are children capable of doing this, they enjoy it.

This is why the term *written language* is preferable to the term *reading*. The term *written language* indicates a situation of true communication in which messages are both received and sent. Such communication is within the reach of young children using computers.

We can go one step further. For young children, using a computer puts them in the position of using writing before reading. This is not only true practically but also theoretically: It is wrong to consider motor coordination a part of reading readiness. In fact, motor coordination is no longer a prerequisite. When using computers, children are in a position to type words, which they then are able to read. Furthermore, experience has shown children love speaking about the pictures they have produced on the screen and the stories they have invented. They then want to write the stories they have spoken. The formula describing this process is:

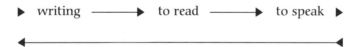

For years educators have discussed whether to teach children using global methods, analytical methods, or mixed methods. These questions become obsolete when using a computer. In fact, when a child types a letter, the child is taking an analytical approach, but choosing a word from a book or seeing the entire word printed on the screen is a global approach. Both approaches are linked and interactive.

When children observe the letters they write as the letters appear from left to right on the screen, then children are building their own structure of space, learning left-to-right directionality and correct letter order. They seldom reverse letters (write them backward). Therefore, it is not necessary to develop these abilities before starting to teach a child how to read. These abilities will develop as the child uses the computer.

What We Know About the Voice Synthesizer

Now that the computer can speak, it becomes alive for the children. Personalizing the computer is not a problem. Children see the mechanical voice as different from a human voice (Cohen 1992a), and they accept it very easily. It also makes them aware that messages exist outside human beings.

This new source of information gives power and independence to children. As letters, words, and sentences are pronounced by the machine, children have a new means to learn, to detect by themselves their own mistakes. Positive feedback is not only visual but also auditory. The auditory feedback is a new source of joy for the children, and it has been proven that positive auditory feedback increases the speed and accuracy of acquisitions (Dahl 1990).

Phonological awareness, which is considered essential in the process of learning to read, is obtained systematically. Thus, reading with the help of a voice synthesizer develops a positive attitude towards reading.

The formula becomes:

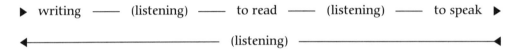

This formula gives the oral feature of the language its whole meaning at each stage of the learning process. Theoretically, we can now ask whether reading is really a silent process, as some authors claim.

What We Know About Language and Languages

Using a computer in a classroom in self-service mode allows for cooperative work. The computer corner is always crowded, and the interactions are more important there than in any other activity. Children help each other. Those who need an explanation ask those who know the answer. They discuss their common projects. When the computer shows there is a mistake, they cooperate to find the right answer. Children become self-sufficient. Never has the expression *freedom to learn* been more true.

We now switch from a teaching situation, where the teacher decides which actions to take, to a real learning situation where the children explore, exchange ideas, and build their own knowledge by interactions with the computer and with their environment.

There is no need for all children to adhere to the same pattern or pace of learning. The problem is not to decide what methods the teacher should use to teach reading, but rather what environment to create to allow children to learn and acquire reading.

In this learning situation, children do not consider mistakes frustrating, but opportunities to search and find answers they need to know. This becomes a pleasant game, because success is always at the end of the road.

Summary

Using new technologies opens new horizons and new challenges. Teachers should accept the fact their role is changed. New types of teacher training are needed, based on the fact that the educational world is changing, and changing fast. Children now live in an ever-changing computerized world, where text, pictures, and voice combine to offer fascinating, new learning opportunities. The source of information is no longer the teacher only, and the children must be prepared to seek and acquire information on their own, using databases and working with students sometimes located far away from their own classrooms. The concept of place and time in education has radically changed. Multimedia and networks are the present conditions in everyday life which education cannot ignore.

For young children the use of computers is an exciting activity. The computer is a powerful tool for discovery, learning, and self-growth. It is also the only way to be prepared, to face and to later integrate, with ease, confidence, and success, the changing world.

Let us not forget that the target population in the research described here consists mainly of children who are generally considered candidates for school failure. Questioning the learning theories was certainly a challenge in itself, but preventing school failure and illiteracy was an even greater challenge. All countries, even the so-called developed ones, face the problem of school failure and illiteracy. All strategies used until now have failed; but research shows that using technologies at an early age, before children become candidates for school failure, can indeed make a significant difference.

The challenge is great. We must face it.

The issues are therefore not only educational but social, political and human. One of our main conclusions when working with young children is that new technologies are an important factor for promoting equity among all children.

Chapter 4

A Computer Corner for Three-Year-Old Children

Gloria Medrano, Ph.D.
Maria Luisa Herrero Nivela, Ph.D.
Department of Psychology and Sociology
School of Education at Huesca
University of Zaragoza, Spain

Young children show us that their ability to learn knows no bounds. With new tools, the right hemisphere of the brain, which is concerned with nonverbal, spatial, creative processes, is activated, and they learn more quickly then we imagined. In 1946, Arnold Gesell and Frances L. Ilg published *The Child from Five to Ten*. In this book, Gesell and Ilg said five year olds are only capable of printing some letters of their first name and they only pretended to read books. The research reported here shows that three year olds write and read; they do not have to pretend. There is no ceiling on children's ability to learn.

Introduction

The present project is being conducted in the context of research being done at the Department of Psychology and Sociology at the School of Education in Huesca, Spain (University of Zaragoza). It constitutes part of a larger project that unites theoretical interests with a search for practical applications that may help optimize children's development through educational interventions.

We have focused our research on children aged three to six because we feel this time of life is one of the most promising stages with respect to developmental potential. Nonetheless, it is also one of the most neglected periods, with respect to systematic research and knowledge about educational interventions that might foster and enrich children's development.

It has been customary to describe the psychological characteristics of children up to the age of six as a function of what they still are not able to do instead of what they are already able to do well. This view has severely limited the range of learning opportunities children have been offered.

Educational thinking at the beginning of this century committed the error of considering the child a small adult and thus forced children into a process of development and learning. One of the main contribution of the psychologists of the 103-s was to make clear that children are not simply small adults and that childhood is not just a period of preparation, but a period of realization of its own. This realization helped to create respect for children's personalities and peculiarities, but also fostered an attitude of limiting the children in realizing their own potential.

To some extent, this is also true of the work of Piaget and his followers. In Piaget's view, development leads to or is a prerequisite for learning. As a consequence, the logical or educational attitude is to wait for development to take place. Questions relating to the possibilities of very small children and early learning have received very little attention, presumably out of fear that learning at a specific stage might occur too early and interfere with the developmental process.

During the last couple of years, ideas quite different from Piaget's have entered the debate. These are the ideas of the Russian psychologist Vygotsky. According to Vygotsky, higher-level psychological processes are first shared between individuals, and it is only through the process of internalization that the processes become part of a single person's mental organization. The influence of the child's interaction with adults or peers is, therefore, crucial for the development of his cognitive structures. (This was also recognized by Piaget and his followers.) Nonetheless, a very basic summary of the Vygotsky approach is: Learning leads to development. As a consequence, the appropriate educational attitude is intervention. This view leads us to stress early learning and to recognize the potential of very young children.

The approaches of Piaget and Vygotsky are not irreconcilable. Rather, they seem to be complementary; both make suggestions that are likely to enrich the educational process. The important conclusion that can be drawn from the contrasting approaches seems to be that development and learning are intimately related processes. The level of development favors the acquisition of specific knowledge and skills; at the same time, a certain level of knowledge and skills, possibly enhanced by an adequate learning environment, activates the development potential of young children.

Early Learning

We would like to clarify the concept of early learning because it plays an important role in diagnosing and fostering the possibilities of very young children. This clarification is divided into two aspects: qualitative and quantitative.

Qualitative Aspects of Early Learning

The concept of early learning is related to notions like early stimulation, compensatory instruction, and the care for mentally handicapped children.

Early learning pertains to what we might call the "normal" slice of the population of children (that is, to children who do not suffer from any difficulties that might inhibit their development). There are some doubts and misconceptions about this term. This is because, quite erroneously, early learning has been linked to excessively pushing the processes of development and learning in very young children. However, the main idea of early learning, as we understand it, is to give children the opportunity to enjoy learning.

In contrast, the basic idea of early stimulation is to help children overcome limitations that stem from a variety of causes. Thus, early stimulation means to fill gaps. This requires the use of compensation strategies. In some cases, in order to overcome a child's limitations, compensation strategies might create situations that may be very demanding on the child.

Early learning does not aim to overcome limitations but to help develop possibilities. Therefore, it does not push children's development by force, but tries to foster development.

Quantitative Aspects of Early Learning

The concept of early learning is related to the first years of human life. However, its use need not be restricted to the first years, nor is this the case for the application of the underlying ideas. To explain this, we would like to introduce a term that has to do with the joy of learning, that is, the joy of learning at the appropriate time.

Why do we talk of early learning and also speak of learning at the appropriate time? Making it possible for children to experience the joy of learning at the appropriate time means offering children the corresponding learning opportunities earlier than such opportunities traditionally have been offered to children. This means offering learning opportunities to children at a stage that educators have traditionally considered too early for a particular learning task. However, the stage is not too early with respect to the actual abilities of the children to learn.

Learning does not occur in the same way in various stages of development. These variations are what establish essential differences between early learning and later learning. These differences are related to two aspects: a temporal aspect and a structural one.

Temporal Aspect

Because early learning precedes later learning, there is no doubt that the former leaves certain traces which, to some extent, predetermine the latter. Early learning is fundamental and influences later learning. Obviously, this influence may be positive or negative, that is, early learning may foster motivation and interest for later learning, or it may do just the opposite.

Structural Aspect

Differences between early and later learning may also be attributed to neurophysiological causes. The brain is particularly impressionable directly after birth, and as a result of environmental influences, neural connections are established on a large scale soon after birth. However, the individual's innate potential requires appropriate environmental stimulation for optimal realization. When the brain is in a state of maximal impressionability, both external and internal stimulation are of prime importance in determining each child's developmental possibilities.

Therefore, the difference between early learning and later learning is critical, because the former establishes neural structures which, to a large extent, determine later learning. (The reverse, in general, is not true.)

Implications for Educators

If we ignore the enormous possibilities of very young children, we commit a serious error that will have considerable negative effects on the educational process:

- Children will lose their original learning strategies.
- Children will start to develop a lack of confidence in their potential.
- Educators will assume that learning strategies must be taught like any other material.

There is no doubt that children have the ability to develop efficient learning strategies at a very early age, if they are given the opportunity to do so. What is more, children at a very early age enjoy doing the things that help them develop learning strategies. We will discover this if we open ourselves to the rich source of information based on observation of their behavior.

If, however, educators at home as well as in school do not have confidence in the possibilities of children, then they will come to block the children's personal capacities. Then the wide range of strategies that children are able to employ will progressively disappear. This lack of confidence on the part of educators will make children believe their personal strategies are not efficient and their main task consists in trying to find out what their teachers want. (That is, children will strive to discover which answers their teachers expect and which strategies their teachers want students to copy. They will do this for little reward, nothing more than the feeling that their teachers consider these responses adequate.)

We definitely should abandon the idea that work is something we do only because we are forced to and that work requires a great deal of effort that we would prefer to avoid. A piece of work done well elicits pleasure. For very young children, the "work" of learning is a pleasure they seek. The satisfaction that results from successfully completing a task that has required some effort is an experience we should not deprive our young ones.

In order to be efficient, each educational process needs to be personal, that is, it should arise from the initiative of the subjects, from their own and original way to respond to the learning task. This is our point of view with respect to the acquisition of learning strategies in the context of educational processes. The teaching of learning strategies might, however, simply result in the introduction of just another superstructure to the students' curriculum, replacing one way of learning mechanically with another. If, up to now, students have been acquiring knowledge without understanding it, they will now apply strategies of learning without knowing why.

All this does not imply that teachers will have to work less, but that they will have to give second thoughts to the way they prepare their classes. As Philippe Meirieu (Meirieu 1991) pointed out, all instructional processes will have to start with the subjects and their reality, aiming at enriching their competence and capabilities and helping them to develop new strategies. The strategies of children may have to be replaced by more efficient ones, but this should not be done without first acknowledging the existing strategies. It is then the task of the teacher to suggest, observe, and regulate the activities of students.

It is therefore important to discover children's first strategies, to foster and help them develop these from early on, bearing in mind that each child is a unique person. We should also realize that children, even when they are very young, participate in activities that are much more complex than traditional child psychology is willing to recognize. We should therefore be or make ourselves aware of

- the enormous potential of very young children and the risk that this potential will diminish if children are not given the opportunity to develop it;
- the differential aspects that developmental stages introduce to learning processes, particularly the special importance of the first stages of life;
- the central role of individual learning strategies and the capacity of very young children to develop these;
- the existence of individual differences and the need to accept these individual differences as an expression of the richness and variety of human nature;
- the value of committing errors as milestones in learning processes; and
- the fact that learning is and should be an act of joy.

The Computer Corner: Objectives

For the reasons given above, the main pedagogical objective of this project is to focus, in Vygotsky's terms, on the zone of proximal development in children. To achieve this, a computer corner was established in a classroom; in this corner the children may use computer programs written by members of our team on child education.

The assumption is the computer corner will act as a catalyst of individual development and will foster

- interaction among peers;
- capability for autonomous learning;
- skills to express comprehension of concepts learned;
- positive evaluation of errors;
- development of spatial mental structures;
- cultivation of learning strategies, especially of metacognitive strategies, discriminative attention, and symbolic thinking;
- the skill to discover meaning in written messages;
- ability to handle fragile material carefully;
- desire to do something well; and
- development of attention to one's own rhythm of learning.

To help children realize their potential, the computer corner must meet the following criteria:

- The computer corner should be integrated into the dynamics of the classroom, it should not disturb it.
- The computer lab should provide impetus to the development of the child as a person.
- It should help children become computer users without unnecessary crutches.
- It should foster collaboration with peers, with maximum independence from adults.

Observational Objectives

A second objective of the study is to use the particular setting that is created by the computer corner to study children's cognitive development at a microgenetic level. This will be accomplished using observational methods.

The dynamics of the computer corner are expected to show evidence of some of the prerequisites that Inhelder and Céllerier (Inhelder and Céllerier 1992) established as indispensable for studying cognitive processes. According to these authors, tasks given to children should present difficulties that

- are real,
- make sense,
- represent a problem,
- may be controlled by the subjects.

In addition, to allow observers to analyze processes of interaction, the situation should

- allow for group activities and
- enhance tutoring processes among children.

Program Development Objective

A third objective of the project is to develop a program to use for training future teachers with respect to teaching and to organizational problems. By observing and analyzing the dynamics that develop among young children in the computer corner, students of the School of Education will acquire knowledge about

- the use of observational methods,
- the potential of very young children, and
- possibilities for organizing the classroom.

Materials and Procedure

Team Infantile Education and Technology created specific software, which is structurally very simple. It is designed to reflect appropriate interests and needs of young children.

The interactions between the children and the computer and among the children and their peers in the computer corner were videotaped using a portable camera. Children became accustomed to this very quickly and even enjoyed it. Videotaping their activity made it possible to review the experiences and to use them as a teaching tool.

Results

We are still comparing the cognitive processes of children who were exposed to the computer corner to those of the children who were not. So far, we have found that spatiality [estructuration] is better among children who participated in the study.

At the end of the academic year, all of the three-year-old children could recognize and locate all of the letters on the keyboard. The technique they generally used to do so was analogy with common objects like "the crown" or "the two mountains" for the letter m or "the snake" for the letter s. When there was a peer in the classroom whose name started with a specific letter, the letter analogy built on the name of the child, for example "la de Mar'a" for *m* or "la de Sergio" for *s*. At four years of age, these children can write some words and short phrases; at five most of them can read and differentiate components of words.

Children's Experiences

Tutoring

The computer facilitates cooperative work and helps children to tutor their peers, because the children know they are the ones who control the computer.

This became evident when a three-year-old girl tutored another girl. The tutor showed the other girl how to draw and in the process displayed her own capacity to execute metacognitive processes. The tutor did this by taking the place of the other girl, anticipating her difficulties, and showing the tutor's own strategies to solve particular problems with the software.

For example when the novice had to chose a letter, the tutor was able to organize the novice's perceptions and made suggestions with respect to form: "It is rounded" or "They do not look alike"; or with respect to color: "A bit of yellow." The tutor also helped the novice understand spatial structuring ("This has a line at the bottom," "This is at the top," "This is in the middle"). Finally, the tutor was able to execute self-regulating processes, finding ways not to touch the keyboard (by putting her hands behind her) as long as the novice was working and to touch the keyboard only if she was asked to do so by the adult.

Although there was an expert–novice relationship, the interaction was positive and egalitarian, allowing for feedback in both directions. It is interesting to note how differently an adult would behave in this situation, trying to help the child construct appropriate schemata of knowledge, giving rules, guiding and motivating the child to solve the problem. Without the adult, working on a problem and actually solving it is motivating in itself and holds the child's attention without any external help.

Motivation

The computer provides special motivation for some children. For example, a three-year-old girl from a marginal group (*gitanos*) found special motivation in the computer corner, where she developed a considerable level of expertise. Because of previous experiences, this girl disliked everything to do with traditional school life. Then she was introduced to the computer corner and given a software manual. It was impressive to see how the computer helped her to overcome her dislike for any kind of learning activity and to discover the adventure of reading in an agreeable and motivating way. She was able to remain concentrated on her work for three and a half minutes without any sign of getting tired.

The girl's activities showed she very rapidly was able to automate the processes of organizing; she quickly learned to write an article and to separate it from the noun with a space. She was able to accept her mistakes without frustration and to learn from her errors by making herself aware again of the task and correcting only the part of the solution that contained the error. She was able to execute up to seven steps in a row, which seemed to indicate a rather high-capacity working memory. It was surprising that she was even able to type words that she saw in her working manual, since she could not read nor write before her experience with the computer.

This girl showed not only good perceptual and short-term memory capacity, she also exhibited the first signs of a mode of thinking that was not fast and somewhat mechanical, but that paused between movements to reflect upon the situation and then followed up with some action (touching a specific key, for example). She also began to use strategies of self-regulation, for instance, when she moved her head after noting an error, thinking for a while, and then acting correctly. At the end of a page, she felt satisfied because of the work she did well. She only infrequently looked for approval from the adult.

Systematic Observation as a Research Method

Systematic observation was used as a research method because in working with very young children, only this method reveals the kinds of information that otherwise would not be accessible. The study deals with observations in a natural setting, that is, a classroom with a computer corner, where attention is focused on the processes of teaching and learning that take place in a small group of very young children. The subjects are small children, between three and five years of age. Both their verbal and nonverbal behavior (facial expression, movement of the hands, etc.) are observed. This method of observation makes it possible to collect a large amount of information about the interactions that take place among members of a group working together at a computer as well as about individual cognitive and metacognitive processes of each child interacting with the computer.

Summary

No matter the country or the environment, if you give children the opportunity to learn and prepare a stimulating environment with rich media, children reveal their enormous potentials and learn in a joyful and satisfactory way.

Chapter 5

Computers and Special Needs Students

Once he got the computer, he knew he was in charge of his own learning. When a teacher in school requires him to write on demand, everything shuts off. You give him control and his words just flow. When he writes to other students worldwide online on the "Imagination Network for Kids," he writes the history of where he has been and what he is doing; he writes novels for other kids, the ideas and words never stop. He can adopt different personas, and he is no longer a learning disabled child. For kids with a learning disability, the computer is a must!

Penny Fogel

Computer technology is quickly becoming the most powerful device to help exceptional children with their learning. A student with cerebral palsy speaks his first words by choosing words presented on a computer screen under his control, commanding a speech synthesizer to pronounce the words. Deaf students practice speech sounds with visual representations on the screen. Aphasic children press pictures on a membrane keyboard to communicate with synthesized speech.

Computers offer the most help to children on either end of the educational spectrum, including intellectually gifted on one end and learners who have difficulties with intellectual learning but who have strengths in other areas on the other end.

Hearing Impaired Students

The deaf is one of the largest groups to benefit from the new technology. Video-interactive devices have been designed to teach lip-reading skills. Computers with modems are replacing telephones as communication devices for the deaf.

Communication between the deaf and the hearing world is difficult. The computer can convert normal speech into line configurations. The deaf can learn to talk by matching their own speech patterns to this pattern for a given sound. However, deaf children learn language best by actively operating on it, just as other children do. We need to provide deaf children with computer-based opportunities to play with language in meaningful contexts (Clements 1985).

Debbie has the look of a frustrated mother. Her young daughter, the light of her family and a special gift after two sons, was born bright and beautiful but deaf. Debbie and her husband have done everything in their power to provide a loving, nurturing learning environment at home; they see the great spark of intelligence their daughter has. Now they are looking for a school so she can develop her social skills as well as further her intellectual growth. However, their local school district has little to offer but dismal programs devoid of funds, equipment, technology, expertise, and facilities. Debbie challenges the system, writes the school district, appears before them, becomes a champion for not only her daughter's needs but for those of other children with special learning needs. Her story appears in the local newspaper. I watch this loving mother devote hours to improving the educational system to meet the needs of hearing-impaired youngsters. The strain of this effort is apparent.

Two years later, I meet Debbie in the hall. I inquire about her daughter. Debbie beams as she tells me of the great success her daughter is experiencing, in school and out. Debbie credits much of her daughter's progress to working with Kidworks and the IBM Speech Viewer. Debbie describes how computers have helped her daughter:

> Computers seem ideal for the deaf population. Having a precocious and highly gifted deaf preschooler, I knew I would be using a computer with and for her, but I was pleasantly surprised at the *when* and the impact it had on her, her teachers, and our family. As a brilliant preschooler with little language, Emily was frustrated and withdrawing from people. She was put on the IBM Speech Viewer to see what would happen. Common wisdom was that children younger than five probably wouldn't benefit. That common wisdom … was thrown out fast! In 15 minutes, Emily had mastered the concept of pitch and was responding on cue to make the hot air balloon on the screen avoid mountains and travel through valleys. Pitch is very difficult to master if you can't hear it. This two-year-old was able to put together what was happening on the screen—the visual—with her voice. She was able to make connections far beyond those expected for her age. She was completely mesmerized by this. We practiced loudness, breath control, and starting and stopping, with balloons blowing up, monkeys climbing a tree to get a banana, cars on a racetrack and trains crossing bridges. This was an excellent use of technology for this child. We were allowed to borrow the computer and software to use at home for the summer. It was well used.
>
> The next step was to use technology for cognitive tasks, such as math sorting and matching, and for matching American Sign Language (ASL) hand signs to letters, and word identification. At three-and-a-half years, Emily literally took the mouse out of the teacher's hand before the demonstration was finished.

She then completed three or four games without error while some of the other five year olds were still beginning the first game. This is a child desperately in need of technology. Deaf people continually rely on hearing aids and translators, and they are not often in an environment where they are in control.

Recognizing Emily's innate ability to learn, I was not prepared to accept the average reading level of deaf adults, which is between third and fourth grade.... I was determined to find the best learning tools available for my daughter. Recognizing both her need to be challenged and stimulated and ... [to] read English, we created some computer substitutes and used the Geo-Safari with her. Geo-Safari is a quasi-computer learning tool that uses questions and answers in an interesting format. The user pushes a number for the correct answer. It is relatively inexpensive and completely visual.... My daughter does read now and is able to use some of the premade Geo-Safari cards. I am making some with sign language and pictures to print cards for her....

Emily's favorite computer programs are the ASL dictionary with the concentration game; KidWorks 2 for writing and painting (I have observed that she sees connections visually that she can't express orally); Bug Book, which is also a painting program; Reader Rabbit; and an assortment of CD-ROM programs provided by her preschool teacher. Hearing aids and an auditory trainer help her only a little. The computer holds great promise for her and others like her. I am quite sure that she will continue to benefit from computers and technology as she gets older.

One of the problems we did encounter was that many of the new software programs use auditory instructions and/or signals, which are useless for the deaf. I hope software developers will consider the needs of deaf children and design appropriate materials for them.

Nonvocal Children

One of the pioneers in working with young children with special needs and the talking computer is Dr. Laura Meyers. Working in the University of California, Los Angeles, Department of Pediatrics as the language consultant to the toddler classroom of the UCLA Intervention program, she met young children who could not talk. She had been searching for a system that would give them a means to communicate when she met Ricky. At two years old, he was one of the most severely physically handicapped youngsters she had ever met. Yet, as she observed Ricky at play, she saw the joy of life in his eyes. Then and there she decided she must help him. In conversations with his teachers, she learned about communication devices that light up when you move a switch, but these devices were designed for older children and adults, not toddlers. The teachers planned to teach Ricky how to swallow and crawl, but they did not plan to help him learn to communicate. When Meyers discovered this, she borrowed a speech synthesizer and showed it to Ricky. With great difficulty he finally was able to position his hands to push the squares. After 10 minutes, when Meyers tried to take away the speech synthesizer, Ricky wrapped his body around it so tightly she could hardly take it from him. She promised him she would get one for him.

Her next step was to start talking to people about computers. All of the communications devices available at the time were too difficult for Ricky. Meyers ultimately designed her own system, called Programs for Early Acquisition of Language (PEAL). This system was unique in that it had a flat, touch-sensitive membrane board with large squares for pictures, symbols, and words. The board was connected to an Apple II computer equipped with an Echo II speech synthesizer. Plastic overlays were designed so that the pictures over the squares could be changed.

With the prototype, Meyers began a research study designed to learn whether children would be more responsive when they controlled either the graphics or the speech. Her hypothesis was that two-year-olds would prefer speech because it's developmentally meaningful—they're trying to learn to talk. She felt that the graphics may be fun and games, but speech is speech. What Meyers found was children as young as 20 months old already thought they had failed; they knew they were not talking and knew that people were disappointed in them. She found that the computer immediately gave them the ability to communicate verbally. In many cases, with that success, the children started talking with their mouths.

Language springs essentially untaught from a child's sense of his or her ability to take part in a human dialogue and as the child tries to make sense and interact with the world. When children are successful at this task, their language grows at an amazing rate because they know they can do it. What the computer can do for other children is provide them with the early success that allows them to risk further literacy.

Too often, educators, especially those working with special education students, feel they must teach many basic subskills before the special child will be able to write or read. They teach isolated sounds, handwriting, grammar, and punctuation. For children who have difficulty controlling their bodies or focusing their minds, this approach convinces them they will always be failures; it is tantamount to encouraging them to give up. Early experiments in this area began to show researchers that perhaps some early skills-and-drills methodology and primitive communication tools, like the pencil, might be responsible for the lack of early literacy in these children. For years, the children themselves had been blamed as handicapped learners. Fortunately, some dedicated researchers saw the gleam of intelligence and the great desire to be understood in each child. Researchers like Laura Meyers found the tools that helped these children tell their stories and control their learning as they had never before been able to do.

Besides working with toddlers at UCLA, Meyers taught graduate courses at the University of Southern California in computers for young children and also worked at the City of Hope with teenage students with Down syndrome. One student, David, had been diagnosed with Down syndrome when he was very young. His parents had been told he would never be able to learn much more than self-help skills. He was presently attending a school for severely handicapped youngsters. David's parents brought him to see Meyers at City of Hope, and she began working with him using the computer with speech. One day, David wrote a letter inviting his teacher aide to have lunch with him at McDonalds. David had a crush on his instructional aide. After he typed his letter, David listened to the computer read it to him. He beamed with pride as he heard the message he had composed. When Dr. Meyers asked him if he intended to give the aide the letter, he nodded his head. She told him they would print it out. With the printed invitation in hand, a proud, beaming David left the session. Obviously, David could accomplish more than just self-help skills. Dr. Meyers said it made her angry to see how human beings are pigeonholed when, with new tools and new knowledge about literacy, they can far exceed meager expectations.

Meyers discovered through her studies that nonvocal children have an intrinsic motivation to learn.

> We've found children as young as 20 months already think they've failed. They already know they're not talking. They already know that people are disappointed in them.

> What we can do is immediately give them the ability to talk through the computer. And what happens in many cases is that they start talking with their mouths. At first they thought, "I'm a failure, I can't talk." And all of a sudden they think, "I can." And the words just start to come out (Meyers 1984).

The unique thing about the PEAL program and the subsequent Talking Textwriter program, written by Meyers and associates, was its focus giving control to the child. (Other software programs at this time were drill programs or computer aided instruction programs, to which children responded like drones, punching keys and receiving messages like *Wrong!* Try again.") For children with very little control over their lives, being in control was a great gift. After working with many students, Meyers concluded that, with the language skills that computer-enhanced training provides, people with disabilities can achieve much more than anyone expected. Disabled students know they have a problem with language, and they know when they are given this new tool that it will help them learn to communicate. Because they know how important communication is, the promise of success in this endeavor is a great relief to them. The computer voice empowers children to participate in speaking and writing. It allows them to participate in the human dialogue. Technology allows these youngsters to enter the mainstream on their own. It finally gives them some control over their environment.

Orlando is one of those children.

Orlando was in a classroom in South Texas. When he entered the computer lab, the aide told the teacher, "This is Orlando, he is LEP (Limited English Proficient) and has Down syndrome. He can't do anything, but you have him for this morning in your Writing to Read lab." Maria Gonzalez, the teacher, loves a challenge. On his first written paper Gonzalez noticed the shape of the sun. Recognizing this early sign of literacy (the sun was one of the first messages primitive humans drew on cave walls), she smiled at Orlando and asked him if he had drawn a sun. He nodded and smiled in response. Recognizing that Orlando was in the silent stage typical of young second-language learners, Gonzalez did lots of smiling, nurturing talk, and praise. In his next writing Orlando drew many suns. Although his eye–hand coordination was very limited, Orlando began to experience success on the keyboard. He typed his name and also the words he saw displayed around the classroom. When he took his paper back to his desk, he noticed he had written *yello* for *yellow*; with his pencil, he added the *w*. At five and a half years, Orlando had just edited his own work. By May, this boy (who they said could not do anything) was writing sentences. His confidence in himself as a learner was evident. Orlando's work shows us the potential within every child. For the first time we are finding ways to help Orlando and children like him experience success in school.

Gifted Children

When the exceptionally gifted child goes to school, problems often occur. To the very bright child, school places obstacles in the way of learning, perhaps for the first time. Some children attempt to please adults by rigidly adhering to the system's requirements; some withdraw; others rebel and become disruptive. In every case there is real damage to their attitudes, learning patterns, and abilities (Webb 1982). Schools are often geared to teach the norm; most competencies are based on the grade level or average child. Gifted children must be allowed to explore and achieve at their own level, a level often higher than the teacher. This is a real challenge to the educator. Using computers helps educators meet the intellectual, creative, and personal needs of the gifted child. Computers allow these children to write their own stories and reports and also achieve the interpersonal skills they need. (They accomplish the latter by working with groups of children on creation of computer media programs.)

Matthew and Nicholas, two first graders, collaborated on the story that appears in figure 5.1. These bright boys would never have been able to create this outstanding story without the assistance of the computer. Figure 5.1 offers their story exactly as they collaborated and wrote it, minus the illustrations.

A strong self-concept is vital for gifted children. Often, they are neglected because it is assumed other children need to be attended to first. However, high intelligence does not guarantee emotional or social intelligence. The gifted child often feels different, isolated, weird, and left out. Good teachers who attend to their needs, plus technology that assists them in construction of their own learning, are very important to their success.

Libby's Story

Libby was five years old and in kindergarten. She was reading *Little Women* at home when she entered school. No one asked her parents or her if she could read. She was quite bored the first day of school with the slow pace of learning. After a couple of weeks of long hours of boredom, her class was taken to the writing environment of a word processing lab. In this environment Libby could write using a pen, pencil, marker, computer … whatever she chose. Here Libby put down on paper all the ideas she had been daydreaming about her first weeks of school. She wrote and wrote and wrote every day. Once she wrote a story about a little girl who observed two older teens kissing; after three pages she wrote, "there's more to this story." She edited her work as she re-read it to herself. Finally, after five descriptive pages written about a romance (including words like *skinny dipping*, she ended her story with the words, "it is not troo!" For a five year old, she had a marvelous sense of story.

Nicholas Top Gun
illustrated by Matthew written by Nicholas

I had a rocket that goes 1000 feet up in the sky. If you had one of these you would go waco ok. I want to tell you a story about jets. Wants I had a rocket that youstoo bellong to the Army. The Army took it and I went with it. They had 10000 000 jets. They even had the f14. All of them had 5000 000 000 000 missells in them the size of the sillver bullet. The Navy had the same things as the Army. The Navy had 270000 tanks so did the Army. There was 1,0000,000 men. The men had bazookas, rifles and bombs. I was in the war too. My rocket blew up a jet. BOOOOOOOOM! The Man that was in the jet blew up. The Navy took the guns and bombs and evrey thing they had. The Navy had wun that war but the Army will win the next time. You will see the next war. The Army is a good team. The Navy is a good team to. My rocket did blow up when my rocket blew up that jet. A war came agin. Tanks were out. Jets were flying to. The war couldn't be stopped. Many got kiled. I axudentley sneezed and I had a mach in my hand. The mach cot on fire and I dropped it. The ground was on fire. I was trapped! It was terubel. My Mom and Dad went to my funeral when I dide. The Army was sad to but the Navy was happy cowubungu dood they said tubyubloor dood they said a lot of funny words. You no there was a lot of wars. Another war came and this time it couldn't be stopped. The Army was wining that war. The Navy saw a air craft kereeer with jets and tanks and other stuff that they kere kereeer. The kereeer is a fierce fighter and a-6E INTRUDER went out to fight. The instruder got bloon up by the PANAVIA TORNADO. peace chapter 2 The Navy said let there be peace umung us all there was peace for a little wille for that little while the men went home. Hint if the peace brakes the earth will blo up if the earth blose up they will dy and the story will end.Or the F-7 night hok will save the day. I no that the F-7 Night hock will save the day. Air kraft keeerers because they are big! things. the would fit the siz of 3 big buses the buses are big. Back To The War. the war is a dangerous thin to live whith. The peace was broken now the world didin't blow up. But the world was geting beet up. If the earth will blow up it will fail.

chapter 3 name of jets.
hot wings 2
F-5 TIGER II
FB-111
AV-8B HARRIER II
A-6E INTRUDER
AH-64 APACHE
PANAVIA TORNADO
B-1B BOMBER
A-10 THUDERBOLT II
T-38 TALON
A-7 CORSAIR II

Figure 5.1   Nicholas Top Gun

Advantages of Computers for All Children

1. Computers are motivating, they are fun. All of us love challenges and love to make things happen.

2. Computers with good software can be highly interactive as opposed to books, tapes, films, radio, and television. With a computer, the user controls what happens.

3. Computers are nonjudgmental and they have infinite patience. You can work slowly or rapidly, it does not make faces or criticize. It never gets tired and crabby.

4. Computers with hypermedia can not only explain concepts in a more interesting, visual or animated manner, but can respond to inquiries in various ways, depending on how the user chooses to access materials.

5. Computers can simulate situations too complex, dangerous, or costly to do in the classroom. Chemical reactions, ecosystems, space travel, and such can safely be explored.

6. Using Hyperstudio and other authoring systems, children can create reports and research for their peers. It is in problem solving and in the creation of these materials that real-world learning occurs.

7. Through telecommunication, computers bring the resources of the world into the classroom and allow students in one classroom to communicate with others anywhere in the world.

8. Computers foster the writing process by making editing and creating materials much easier. They also make the final product look professional.

Early-Intervention Programs

Reading Recovery is an early-intervention program for young readers who are experiencing difficulty in their first year of reading instruction. The program is designed to serve the lowest achieving readers in a first-grade class. Reading Recovery was developed by New Zealand educator and psychologist Dr. Marie M. Clay. Now a national program in New Zealand, Reading Recovery is also receiving much attention in the United States and Canada. Currently, teacher leaders in Ontario, Arizona, Ohio, South Carolina, Texas, and California are training classroom teachers and administrators in Reading Recovery procedures. In Reading Recovery, children receive individual daily lessons from a specially trained teacher. Reading Recovery has gathered good results in bringing individual students to the level of their peers (DeFord 1991). The program's primary goal is to prevent failure and to help children become independent learners before their misunderstandings about reading are habituated into patterns of reading failure. This is the same benefit the talking computer provides.

Visit to Maungawhau School in Auckland

Maungawhau District School in Auckland, New Zealand, has as its school motto, "It is tone that makes music." In every classroom in this outstanding school, the tone was evident. It was one of enthusiasm for learning, where all learners were producers rather than consumers. Educators in the United States often give lip service to this concept, but it was a reality at Maungawhau. In every classroom students constructed and expressed their own literacy through art, books they created, or oral presentations about their lives and writings.

There are two major populations at this school: New Zealanders and Maori, or early New Zealanders. Because second-language students or special education students are not identified or considered problematic, they are not, and *all* are learning. Reading Recovery is a fundamental program at this school. How important was it? The assistant director of the school was also the Reading Recovery teacher.

In an individual Reading Recovery session with a Maori child, the child received an impressive amount of individual attention, support, enthusiasm, and encouragement. If it were practicable to teach all children in this manner, many educational problems would disappear. Though most students in the program are successful, those with limited eye–hand coordination are unable to copy and write. Learning of the talking computer, the Reading Recovery teacher agreed it might be a valuable addition to the program. This is the type of adjustment professional educators must practice when adapting any type of methodology to a particular student. In this setting and others, the computer could help support literacy development in a more cost-effective manner than one-on-one teaching affords.

Success of Reading Recovery is not limited to New Zealand. Smith-Burke and Jaggar, reporting on implementing Reading Recovery in New York, present evidence that shows a large portion of children who receive Reading Recovery instruction become successful readers. Nevertheless, it is abundantly clear that Reading Recovery alone is not sufficient to address the critical issues facing schools today, particularly urban schools (Hiebert 1994). What is needed is a comprehensive approach to early literacy instruction; the talking computer should certainly be a component of this approach.

Summary

In *Learning Denied*, Denny Taylor (1991) does an outstanding job of telling the story of a young child whose educational experiences and literacy development were hampered by early assessment and erroneous labeling by a school. The school not only did not recognize many elements of Patrick's literacy, but its response to perceived problems virtually denied Patrick's abilities and, in a certain sense, Patrick himself.

Rather than wasting time on what label to call the students, let's call them children who want to learn, and find the environment for learning that helps them the most. This approach puts questions about the nature of the children's educational problems and the best methods for solving them far ahead of questions about causation. In fact, this approach maintains that information about the cause of a child's academic deficiencies are of little if any help to an educator faced with the task of remediating the deficiencies. By de-emphasizing standardized tests and emphasizing continuous evaluation and observation of a students' performance in the classroom and substituting the use of negative labels with the use of powerful learning tools, we can be of much more help to all learners especially those with difficulties (Coles 1987).

To students, a label is an obstacle to learning; to educators, it is all too often an excuse to push the child into a corner or box. New Zealand schools don't label their Maori children LEP; they don't label students with short attention spans ADD. Indeed, as the director of the Maungawhu School observed, "You Americans separate your children by placing many labels on them—and cause yourselves many problems. We accept all children as the learners they are. We expect them all to work to the best of their abilities—and they do!"

In a learning environment that provides the tools children need to learn, all children—regardless of their position on the educational spectrum—can achieve success.

Chapter 6

Writing to Read

The computer can give the learner the world's most beautiful feeling, the Greek "Eureka:" I got it, I know it, I can see it, I can understand it! That's a transforming feeling; to be awakened from dormancy, from sadness to strength, to dignity. I can write, I can read!

John Henry Martin

Writing to Read (WTR) is an early literacy program developed in the early 1980s by John Henry Martin, an educator with 35 years experience in elementary education. Based on a compilation of most current educational research on early literacy, especially the work of Piaget, Bruner, Orton, Fernald, Montessori, Chall, Chomsky, and Dewey—and including 50,000 hours of research on talking typewriters and the development of the talking computer—this innovative program, now called Writing to Read 2000, has been helping kindergarten and first-grade students across the nation write and read in their own natural language. As recently as 1988, more than 1 million preschoolers, kindergartners, and first graders had already experienced WTR in more than 5,000 labs and classrooms in schools throughout the United States (Grimm 1988).

While participating in the program, children learn the sound/letter associations needed to write what they can say and to read what they have written. In *Writing to Read*, Martin (Martin and Friedberg 1986) explains the reason he sold his ideas to IBM was that they were the only computer hardware company or publisher willing to accept his insistence on adequate testing (Martin and Friedberg 1986). IBM agreed not to sell Writing to Read to school systems until research had been conducted, initially with 1,000 children over five years and with 10,000 children across the nation. Most products are marketed to the school market with testing on a small sample of 15 children or, possibly, the children of the developers. The amount of time, money, and research put into this program before it was sold to the schools was exemplary. Martin stated, "Only IBM saw the wisdom and need to protect the children of America from computer products and procedures that were experimental and largely untested. They subjected the Writing to Read System to rigorous field testing in 1982, then extended their commitment for an additional year while the Educational Testing Service confirmed, in a study of 10,000 children, that the results indicated that this method of teaching writing and reading to kindergarten and first grade children was superior to a degree not matched by any other system" (Martin and Friedberg 1986). Writing to Read is probably one of the most well-researched technology programs to date.

For the past 10 years evidence has been building that the computer is essential. The computer needs to become an everyday tool present in every classroom and integrated into all curriculum areas.

Features of Writing to Read

The Marriage of Phonics and Whole Language

Technology may be a bridge between those who for endless years have haggled over the efficacy of Phonics Only versus Whole Language. Frozen at either pole of the argument, they have been unable to envision a classroom environment in which each child learns to read in a meaningful, natural manner with exactly the right combination of writing, reading for interest, and phonics. If nothing else, technology should prove to educators that language experience can work for all students when they process their own language with a word processor.

Appropriate integrated phonics instruction can be imbedded in this process. Writing to Read focuses on the writing process but also recognizes research that supports the inclusion of phonemic awareness. Phonemic awareness can be used to predict reading achievement (Juel 1988, Lomax and McGee 1987, Lundberg and Peterson 1988). Children who have made the connection between the alphabetic principle and the 42 phonemes of speech usually have success in early reading (Griffith et al 1992).

Literacy-Rich Environment

A vital component of Writing to Read 2000, is the creation of a literacy-rich environment that provides numerous opportunities for writing, reading, speaking, and listening. Using a multiple learning-center approach, the Writing to Read 2000 environment provides opportunities for the engagement of multiple modalities—visual, auditory, tactile, and kinesthetic. The purpose of this program is to enable children to write and read using their own natural language. The major focus of the program is on children's daily writing of their experiences on the talking word processor, but at the same time, the software introduces the alphabetic principle, or the idea that the words can be constructed with sounds, or phonemes, which are represented by letters or combinations of letters (Martin and Friedberg 1986).

New Features

Writing to Read 2000 incorporates a new word processing program to replace the old Primary Editor Plus. This new word processor, called Write Along, incorporates many improvements based on (1) what years of observations show that children most need from technology support and (2) the immense improvement in what the technology can now deliver. The inclusion of a complex draw program helps children convey their messages in many ways. Young, emergent writers do not typically differentiate markedly between drawing and writing to communicate. Both are needed to convey intended meanings. The new version of Writing to Read also includes a capability to pronounce letters and sounds for students when they require this assistance in the process of writing. It allows them to play with fonts and borders and other print options as they prepare their final piece of writing. Most important, it allows them to hear the computer read back what they have written. The feelings of control and excitement encourage them to continue their journey to literacy.

Building on the Language Experience Approach

Of the myriad programs that have been developed to help children learn to read over the past 30 years, the Language Experience Approach has always been the most powerful one for early literacy for learners aged 2 to adult. Telling about our own experiences, dreams, and interests is a primary activity for adults throughout their lives. It is much more interesting to read a story about what is happening to you then be forced to read a dumbed-down story about the day someone's dog ran away. A 50-year-old carpenter learning to read English would have much more interest in writing about his life and reading what he wrote than in reading a pre-primer book. The same is true of children.

The Language Experience Approach is discussed in detail in chapter 2. Though a sound theory, the problem with this approach is implementation. It requires a teacher to take dictation from the learner. This is too time-consuming to be practicable for teachers of 30 students. In addition, the approach conveys the silent message, You cannot write yet; teacher must do this for you.

With a sophisticated word processor replacing the pencil-wielding teacher, this hurdle can be overcome. Learners can type their own thoughts and ideas directly into the computer, see what they wrote, hear what they wrote, and print a copy for imme-diate enjoyment and to be read to all interested parties. This process of converting lan-guage experience stories to print via word processing I call language processing.

Writing to Read 2000 and similar early literacy programs that use technology and learning centers in the classroom can provide students with language processing sup-port throughout the day in all curriculum areas. Weekly one-hour visits to a com-puter lab are not sufficient to allow the power of this writing learning tool to have any lasting effect on learners. This is a tool that must be as available as a pen or a pencil. Writing must be practiced daily in conjunction with reading good literature and classroom discussions and explorations of topics students need to know about or are interested in learning about.

Initial Reactions

Initial reaction to Writing to Read programs received mixed reviews, with educa-tors, such as Slavin, demanding research data to determine its effectiveness (Slavin 1990). Studies were conducted, but the majority used existing reading tests, such as ITBS or CTBS, to measure the results. The results were not conclusive. A major reason for this was that the tests were testing isolated *reading* skills, whereas children using Writing to Read were gaining self-esteem. The children experienced phenomenal writing growth as they used Writing to Read to write their own stories daily, and as they became fluent readers by reading their work to anyone who would listen. Neither of these achievements are measured by existing reading tests.

In an effort to demonstrate to the educational community and test for themselves the effectiveness or lack of effectiveness of the Writing to Read program, six major California School districts joined in a partnership with IBM to obtain the computer equipment. I was hired to write a detailed qualitative evaluation plan and then conduct a two-year evaluation study. Earlier reports (Casey 1984, Goodlad 1984) confirmed the effectiveness of using not only quantitative data but also ethnographic data (collected through interviews, observations, anecdotal records, writings portfolios, and questionnaires) to evaluate a language arts program. This combination of quantitative and qualitative data yields a more accurate picture of what an innovation is accomplishing than does quantitative data alone.

Riordan Foundation

In 1987, lawyer and philanthropist Richard Riordan visited a Writing to Read site and was impressed with the early literacy development he observed. Convinced that early learning and early intervention was essential to bring literacy to all students of Los Angeles, Riordan formed a foundation to help provide computer equipment to schools that were willing to pilot new programs and provide training and implementation for teachers.

Success in Los Angeles

One of the first groups Riordan approached was the Los Angeles Roman Catholic Archdiocese. The Los Angeles archdiocese is the largest archdiocese in the United States, both in terms of territory and population. It spans Santa Barbara, Ventura, and Los Angeles counties. Several of its schools contain large populations of Hispanic and South East Asian (Korean, Vietnamese, and Cambodian) cultural minorities. At first the archdiocese's response was rather cool, but it decided to try out the program. Many teachers came to the first training sessions very reluctantly. However, once the computers arrived in their schools and they had the opportunity to witness their effects, the teachers became strong advocates of the program. After one year, one of the teachers who had only reluctantly agreed to try the program described it as a "miracle."

Nine years later, 160 of the 320 archdiocese schools have computers in the classrooms. According to Sister Agnes Jean Vieno, the archdiocese's Writing to Read coordinator, "All our children can write and read at five. Teachers see what happens when the children are interested, involved, and empowered by the computer, and get very excited. Success of the children makes believers of the teachers. Now the teachers from all the other grades want computers in their classrooms."

Sister Agnes Jean strongly believes that computer technology belongs in elementary schools. "We live in a technology-oriented age. Our society is permeated with computers," she says. "We're all turned on by media. It's natural for little kids to sit down without any fear at all in front of technological components of any kind, including computers, and go ahead and use them as tools. It would be a wasted opportunity if schools did not capitalize on the attraction youngsters feel for computers."

Unlike television or videocassette players, there is something magical about computers, suggests Sister Agnes Jean. "With a computer, you have functions to perform," she explains. "How you use those functions is going to change that piece of media. Either we teach our youngsters to use it well or we're cheating them. Children's ability to get and hold a job in the future is completely dependent upon whether they are computerize.... One of the most important results of the program is the aspect of self-image, the improvement in self-esteem that happens because little kids are largely able to manage a lot of their own learning."

Sister Agnes Jean has a favorite story that sums up her feeling about the power of Writing to Read to inspire confidence in children. In an archdiocese school in the heart of the inner city, in a low-income area, across the street from a housing project, there was a third-grade girl. The girl's father was a drug dealer and her mother was an alcoholic. The child didn't speak. She was depressed, morose. It was very difficult to draw her out. When she came to the school, her language deficiency was total. This school, which gives particular emphasis to children who have speaking language deficiencies, introduced the girl to the computer and allowed her to participate in the Writing to Read program all year. Slowly, in this risk-free environment she began to find the words and letters to describe the feelings she held so tightly inside her.

When Sister Agnes visited the school at the end of the year, the girl was writing a story on the computer. It was a very poignant story, just one of many she had compiled in a writing folder. Not only was the child expressing herself in writing, she was eager to read her story (Holzberg 1990)!

After the introduction of the computers into the kindergarten and first-grade classrooms, the innovation spread throughout the school. Teachers and administrators, seeing the successful implementation of technology in the primary classrooms, wanted this same success for all pupils.

Spreading Enthusiasm

The Riordan Foundation has been involved in statewide implementations of Writing to Read in Mississippi, Rhode Island, West Virginia, Alabama, and Vermont, as well as in California. To date, the Riordan Foundation has participated in funding approximately 1,600 Writing to Read projects in 36 states. Mary Odell, director of the Riordan Foundation, points out that innovative educators, for example, in Illinois, have found resources to fund technology by decreasing the amount of money used to buy large volumes of large textbooks.

Reports from Around the Country

Following are reports from two other Writing to Read sites.

Writing to Read Executive Summary Report
by the University of Mississippi

In 1989, the State of Mississippi launched a multiyear commitment to teach first-grade children to read and write by using IBM's Writing to Read Program (WTR). The project was made possible through cooperative funding from the Mississippi legislature and the private sector, the Riordan and Rord Foundations. Three hundred public elementary schools submitted grant proposals, and 60 were awarded programs for the initial phase. The program was chosen based on its strength in individualizing instruction so that children can work at their own pace and its multi-activity, multisensory approach to learning.

Dr. Jim R. Chambless, Associate Dean and Professor of Educational Leadership, University of Mississippi, and Dr. Martha Chambless, Associate Professor of Reading Education, Arkansas State University, led a team of researchers, 27 Mississippi school principals, and 78 Mississippi first-grade teachers in collecting the data for this report.

Conclusions were that first-grade children who participated in the Mississippi WTR program during the 1989–90 school year made greater gains in literacy skills (writing and reading) than comparable first-grade children who received traditional instruction. The outcome measures used in the evaluation project reflect that the use of the WTR program enhanced the development of essential literacy skills for first graders regardless of socioeconomic status, race or sex.

The efforts of the school administrators and teachers in the classrooms have been translated into increased literacy skills for WTR first grade children.

Writing to Read Report from Juneau, Alaska

IBM contributed 16 computers, software and journals to the Juneau School District. The district provided four classrooms to be converted into Writing to Read Centers, four aide salaries and other materials, and agreed to pilot test the program in four schools with over 300 kindergarten, pre-first, and first-grade students. The Alaska Department of Education supplied the required reading books, the time of a Project Coordinator/Teacher Trainer, and contracted with a consulting firm for an independent evaluator to evaluate the pilot project.

The results of the project indicated that the teachers and students noted the word processing software at the computers as one of the outstanding features of the program. The report concluded that Writing to Read was an effective program for building writing skills among young students. Once again, a program like this that empowers students in their own personal writing process is culture free and equally effective anywhere on the globe. This is an important point, for in the past, educators have made the mistake of using culturally biased test measures to measure reading progress, and often children from areas distant from the test makers environment do poorly. One of my colleagues at University of California was hired as a consultant to the Alaska School District some years ago. Her assignment was to find out why the reading test scores there were so poor. She asked what test they were using to measure children's reading. They showed her the Iowa Test of Basic Skills. It was no wonder the test scores were so low, it is not in an Eskimo child's experience background or knowledge base to have grandparents who live on a farm in Iowa, and many of the questions required that kind of knowledge. This problem does not occur when writing and reading are done with children's own word processing. The only caution there is that portfolio assessment with holistic scoring needs to be used to measure the growth of reading and writing, rather than standardized test scores, such as CTBS or ITBS.

Now, fourteen years after the beginning of this technology innovation for early literacy, I attended a Focus meeting of the Riordan Foundation. Formed eight years ago by then-mayor of Los Angeles, Richard Riordan, this foundation has given $8 million to date to support technology for early literacy in our schools nationwide. I listen to the success stories from the Los Angeles Unified School District and wonder what it will take for us to finally give all our children this opportunity. The labs in L.A. Unified never sit empty; after school and on Saturdays, pre-schoolers and illiterate parents work as a team on joint family literacy projects.

One principal told our group of how she had two new students from Mexico, a nine-year-old boy and twelve-year-old girl, both had never attended school and could not speak any English. She put them in the Writing to Read lab every afternoon beginning in September. By January they both were reading and speaking English at approximately a third-grade level. Principals confirmed that to them Writing to Read was not just a kindergarten or first-grade program, it was a literacy foundation for their school. They insisted that their entire staff of teachers, K–5, attend training sessions for they felt this was the way to begin literacy for all children and then realized the importance of following up the writing and reading explosion of first grade during subsequent school years.

Linda Griggs, Coordinator of the State of Mississippi Writing to Read Project, reported that by this summer, after six years of implementation, the entire State of Mississippi will have early literacy labs. Their test scores and, more importantly, the writing and reading and attitudes of their students have reflected this positive change.

When the leaders of school districts who had used this program for over eight years were asked to give their summary of the most powerful aspect of WTR, their first response was the self-esteem of the child and the belief or attitude that they can be a success at writing and reading, so important for any beginning learner. Next they mentioned that the computer, whether in labs or in the classroom, offered students the opportunity to be completely independent at manipulating and using the technology by themselves. They felt this independence and ability to create their own pace and literacy acquisition was a key to success.

The next strengths they identified were the team building among teachers and parents as the whole community became caught up in the excitement of this technology use. Teachers loved the fact that the writings their students did daily automatically provided outstanding portfolio materials for their assessment use, parents much preferred teachers reporting their students developmental growth through portfolio samples than past use of raw scores and stanines.

Other benefits included that fact that the classroom or technology lab provided a perfect opportunity for oral language development for those children who had not developed much expressive language. They also unanimously agreed that writing among young children flourished because they no longer had to "struggle" to make three-inch-high letters that faced the correct direction. The mechanics of making letters was not a hindrance to their writing and reading any longer. They felt the children involved in this program developed a phonemic awareness or understanding of language that many adults do not have.

Summary

Summarizing 8 years of working with the 1,600 Writing to Read projects in 36 states, Odell cites the following as the major advantages of Writing to Read:

- Provides students tools to build bridges from the spoken to written language.
- Enables students to write what they can say and read what they have written.
- Utilizes the students' natural language base.
- Uses integrated multisensory instructional methods.
- Teaches students to be responsible for their own learning.
- Takes advantage of advances in computer technology.

For inner-city children who might have few positive social interactions and success in their daily lives, many educators feel risk-free, early learning labs make a meaningful difference. In these labs, the children wrote stories daily and were asked to share their stories with as many people as possible. When they read their story to a principal, teacher, parent, or peer, the person was asked to sign the back of their paper. All children had great pride in their writings. All products looked equally professional.

Conclusion

Teachers, educators, grant agencies and all can say what they like about Writing to Read. But the real measure is student learning.

Jessica

In his article, "The Corporate Kindergarten: Writing to Read," Paul Evans (1988) shares five-year-old Jessica's dream and aspirations. This amazing technology that turns kindergarten students into authors frees their inner voices so they can at last be heard. Jessica writes:

The Vois Inside you

One day Jenny seid to her mom I want to do jimnastiks
Her mom seid OK why dont you try out for the Olimpiks? Jennys techer was tuf.
it was the day of the Olimpiks. Jenny was scard when it came to her tern.
The she herd a vois it seid you can do it.
Jenny ran to the beem.
She did a back flip
the vois cep saing you can do it.
Then it came agen you can do it.
She one the Olimpks

(Evans 1988)

All kindergarten and first-grade students have hopes and dreams. Here is a way that they can finally be expressed on paper.

Chapter 7

Software for Early Literacy

I have never met a kindergartner who didn't have a desire to learn to read and a literacy foundation we can build on. Even a child who has had little print exposure at home has gotten meaningful language from family talk and even television. There is something "emerging" within each one. If a child's name is Michelle, and she's beginning to notice or scribble an M, there's a place to start.

Gay S. Pinnell

Five year old Peter works at a computer in his kindergarten classroom. "Let me show you what I can do," he says, and he takes the mouse, points at the KidWorks 2 folder, and opens the program. He then selects the drawing option, picks out a scene, and begins creating an illustration for a story he's composed. Peter is in one of the thousands of classrooms using Apple Computer's Early Language Connections (ELC). Designed for K–2 children, this program integrates Macintosh computers, children's literature, instructional software, and other curriculum materials constructed around thematic units. Though it incorporates principles of a whole language approach, some of the software and activities focus directly on phonics and building sound–letter connections. Research affirms this approach leads to effective acquisition of literacy skills (Anderson 1985).

For years, reading experts have been locked in a debate. One view, represented by Frank Smith in *Understanding Reading*, stresses comprehension (Smith 1988b). Smith sees reading largely as a matter of constructing meaning, of finding patterns in a text that confirm or contradict the reader's expectations. The other view, articulated by Jeanne Chall, focuses on the importance of decoding. In *Learning to Read*, Chall emphasizes that readers must learn the code by which letters, words, and larger units can be transformed from written symbols into meaningful sounds and thoughts (Chall 1983).

Recent work in computer science substantiates Smith's view. For example, Roger Schank's efforts to program a computer to "read" *The New York Times* demonstrates how reading comprehension depends not so much on a complete knowledge of English grammar as on a familiarity with stories and the way they represent the world. The computer learns to recognize patterns, predict outcomes, and validate or revise expectations much as a human reader might. However, the progress of computer science also underlines the importance of decoding skills—Chall's point—because computers add new codes to the repertoire of reading. Finally, a solution to the answer is not either whole language or phonics, but a combination of what each individual child needs to know in order to construct their own literacy, with technology as the tool that empowers them to be successful.

Teachers using ELC report that students write more when they use technology. Pat Robinson, one of the innovative teachers, has constructed a learning environment based upon collaboration, peer support, appropriate technical tools, and motivation. Teachers like her are finding creative, effective ways to incorporate technology into their ongoing efforts to improve education. Findings of the ELC studies showed that children are drawn to technology and are intrinsically motivated to use computers. They are highly motivated to write when they know their compositions and illustrations will be printed out and published for all to see. In one classroom, students wore "publisher" or "editor" ball caps as they worked on editing their work. Students compose directly on the computer and add their own computer generated illustrations (Guthrie and Richardson 1995). Some teachers, reluctant to trust students to compose on the computer, require a handwritten draft first. This is a mistake. Only through watching the responses of children will some teachers finally be convinced that it is the empowerment of the writing on the keyboard that spurs on the writing. If the teacher requires it to be laboriously written out by hand, the joy of the process is lost before it has a chance to begin!

Creative Writing at Its Best with KidWorks 2

First graders at St. Andrew's Episcopal School in Austin, Texas, have plenty to talk and write about, according to Technology Teacher of the Year 1992, Diann Boehm. She reports that using the program KidWorks 2, students write daily and are excited to see their print come to life on the computer. The pictures and icons included in the program feature My Word Box help students make the connection between pictures and words. Best of all, the computer text-to-speech capability enables her students to hear their stories as they are created and also when they are complete. Students learn much about their writing as they intently listen to their sentences read back to them. They want their story to sound right.

Boehm found KidWorks 2 to be instrumental in the following observed changes in the primary students at the school:

- Students' vocabularies increase.
- Students want to write more, and they use many adjectives.
- Students grasp sentence structure and learn parts of speech quickly and easily.
- Students' spelling improves, due to the text to speech option.

Primary students at St. Andrew's used KidWorks 2 for writing stories; creating a rebus; building vocabulary around parts of speech; and creating sound books, cross-word puzzles, and cartoons. Often, after writing was completed and printed, stories were laminated for students to keep and take home. Publishing reinforced the skills the students were learning and gave them a sense of accomplishment and pride in themselves as authors (Boehm 1993).

Hardware and Software Innovations

Writing to Read, published by JHM Corporation and IBM and sold only for IBM computers, was an innovation developed by educators for children. It was backed by years of sound research. The strongest components of Writing to Read were the word processor with speech capability and the incentive it provides children to write daily from their own language experience. To prevent the possibility that the technology would be misused, program creator John Henry Martin established vital practices for use. Often, however, the vital practices were too rigid or misused. For example, one vital practice was having the children rotate among five learning centers with a variety of activities (with computers at only two of the centers). This practice was meant to encourage variety of experience, but in some instances, a rigid teacher or lab aide forced students to leave the word processor in the middle of writing their most profound story because their 15 minutes were up. In addition, the journals IBM provided with the computers looked suspiciously like workbooks that taught isolated skills.

An article about Writing to Read describes how empowered teachers can make curricular innovations. By relating the story of one teacher who redesigned a literacy lab to meet the needs of her students, the authors point out how important the empowerment of the teacher is in adapting curricular innovations to meet the specific needs of the children they serve (Labbo et al 1995). This is the most effective way to implement the new technology.

How Computers Support Learning

What stands out about all the reports on the Writing to Read program, Apple Learning program, and other programs that include the talking word processor for young children is that reading has taken on new meaning and purpose for the students. In the past, reading programs for kindergarten students developed vocabulary slowly, through word recognition, or laboriously, through one sound memorized, at a time. Today, we see kindergartners using vocabulary and story sequence that far exceeds what educators thought was possible from students of such a young age. In the future students will continue to develop these early comprehension skills, grasp new concepts, and attach meaning to writing and reading even earlier in their lives if we afford all of them this valuable learning tool, have faith in their abilities, and encourage their accomplishments.

Seymour Papert points out an important strength of computers that may explain why more children find success using computers than using old tools. According to Papert, one of education's toxins is the imposition of the planned analytic mode of thinking on everyone, whether it fits their personality or not. The U.S. education system has been biased in favor of people who like detail or planning and biased against people who prefer the big picture and unplanned change or discovery learning (Papert 1980). The computer, with certain software, puts the child in control of the environment. For example, the software Logo puts the child in charge when exploring mathematical concepts, and the various talking word processor software puts the child in control when exploring language processing. Such a tool works for both types of children, the planners and the explorers. Sherry Turkle, MIT sociologist and psychologist, studied how the computer affects the way children think. She found different styles of mastery. Hard mastery is the imposition of the child's will through the implementation of a plan. Children who seek hard mastery on the computer are the planners, who have always been in sync with the programmed approach to learning. Soft mastery is a more intuitive style of learning. If hard mastery is for planners and engineers, soft mastery is for artists (Turkle 1984). Many students in special education programs seem to be students who prefer soft mastery; they failed in classrooms where the teacher demanded hard mastery. Appropriate software (not programmed computer-aided instruction) accepts all students, regardless of their style of mastery. Thus, all learners have an equal chance at attaining literacy in their own style.

Business Partnerships

Computer hardware manufacturers have made outstanding efforts in support of education. Both IBM and Apple, in particular, have made large contributions and donations in support of education by including educators on software and hardware development teams, listening to educators, and joining partnerships for educational projects in the schools. These two companies have begun the type of partnerships between business and education so sorely needed to serve the educational interests of the next generation.

More business partnerships must be sought out and entered into by schools. Only a true community–school partnership will be able to produce the technology-rich classrooms needed. Hillary Clinton titled her new book after an old African proverb, "It takes a village to raise a child" (Clinton 1996). The village of today may be an electronic global village, but it is made up of children and parents and grandparents and citizens who all want the same thing, to create for children the better tomorrow which they deserve.

Educators need to keep abreast of the new software and CD-ROM packages being developed daily. The World Wide Web site of the Software Clearing House (http://www.Stan-co.K12.ca.us), developed by Dr. Ann Lathrop, provides reviews of new programs for use in the classroom or at home.

The names of software programs will change rapidly in these days of technology development. However the insightful teacher who recognizes the need to provide a supportive publishing environment in which children can write daily and find their own voice will not become outdated. We need these teachers in every classroom where children are placed to learn.

Cautions About the Use of Computers

Computers can provide a helpful or a traumatic experience, depending on how the teacher handles word-processing instruction (Rosegrant and Cooper 1983). When used as effective tools, computers can encourage exploration and experimentation with language, can empower students, and facilitate communication. However, when a child or teacher misuses the computer's capabilities by overemphasizing correctness of form and content or by becoming overly critical about first drafts, using a computer becomes traumatic. Regardless of the promise of computer technology, word-processing lessons can suffer from the same poor teaching methods as the more traditional paper-and-pencil, textbook writing reading curriculum (Heller 1991).

WiggleWorks: A Beginning Literacy System

WiggleWorks, a new beginning literacy system from Scholastic, could be named Writing to Read and Early Learning Connections meet Reading Recovery. It is a perfect example of how each researcher or developer builds upon another's research. Advisors to this program include Dr. Gay S. Pinnell of the University of Ohio, who was the first person authorized to replicate Reading Recovery in the United States, and Dr. Diane Snowball, a scholar from Australia currently teaching at New York University. The classroom management strategies, the inclusion of phonemic sounds on visual letters that children can use to design their own new words, and the books on tape are very reminiscent of Writing to Read.

The talking word processor is limited to eight lines of text, a serious limitation. How could a child like David, the ADD child (see pages 21–22) write his 26-page story? However, since Scholastic was the innovative publisher of the first Talking Screen Textwriter Program (Rosegrant and Cooper 1983), it is a simple matter to include an unlimited text-to-speech word processor to this system.

It should be remembered that the computer as a tool to write language experience stories needs to be the focus of any early literacy program. The child's recognition that his or her own language can be processed into a book makes the initial connection that then makes reading other author's books an exciting adventure.

WiggleWorks allows children to speak into the microphone at the computer to record their own retelling of a story they have just heard read. This is a very good feature that has not been in any other programs. Another feature called, Create a Performance, allows children to work cooperatively to retell stories or make sound effects and develop performances to share with classmates. WiggleWorks is available only in English at this time, but the program will soon be available in Spanish.

The books included in the program are certainly not Caldecott or Newbery award winner quality and lack the interest level that books like Ezra Jack Keats, *Peter's Chair* had in IBM's Stories and More or Writing to Read. That is not to say that some children won't enjoy moving through the program as designed. But the teacher needs to pick and choose support materials appropriate to the styles of each learner. When previewing software, educators should always question who is in control of the learning. To presuppose that teachers control the skills children acquire is a folly. The tendency to control the number of words presented to young children may result in extremely boring stories. Broderbund's Living Books take advantage of the appeal of Mercer Mayer and other acclaimed children's authors; those stories are much better than stories like *Frog's Lunch* included in WiggleWorks.

Considering that many three and four year olds coming to school will have interacted with Living Books, such as *Grandma and Me* and *Ruff's Bones*, educators will have to be extremely careful not to require these children to complete WiggleWorks simply to allow the teacher to use the program assessment. Once again, the program would drive the curriculum! If WiggleWorks is to be used to help the "kid-watching" teacher support children's early literacy, it will be successful. If it is used as a program to be followed in the exact order presented, needed or not, then it becomes just another program to be "gone through." The success of WiggleWorks depends on whether it is used as a tool to explore written and spoken language or as a techie version of programmed learning. Combined with the philosophy of Reading Recovery, and in the hands of a well trained professional, WiggleWorks can be a good learning tool.

A program note says, "When the purpose is instruction, the teacher certainly needs to know what exactly is being read and why." WiggleWorks seems to focus on the materials as the curriculum informant. Children's writing is used as response and retell, with the child acting more as consumer than creator. If WiggleWorks focused first on the child's language experience and need to know, then moved into literature self-selected by the child (with teacher guidance and instruction as needed), and if the Create a Performance and other features were used for support, then the program might be more effective. Research supports that notion, but classroom results and qualitative data on childrens' literature growth from WiggleWorks' present design needs much additional study.

"It is simply double-talk to ask children to take charge of their own learning and at the same time order them to discover something that can have no role in helping them understand anything they care about or are interested in or curious about" (Papert 1993). If the child's mind is burdened by worry or concern, then being told to watch and respond to *Frog's Story* is of little benefit. Writing a story about "why I don't want to have a baby brother or sister because I am worried my mom won't like me anymore" might do a lot more to promote written language development and help the child solve problems through writing. On the other hand, for a child who saw a frog yesterday, *Frog's Story* might just be the right thing to promote interest in reading. The flexibility to meet the needs of each child is a critical component of any learning environment. Frank Smith articulates it best: "Learning is a continuous process, a natural state of the brain, and children therefore are likely to be learning all the time. Children do not need to be taught that they can learn" (Smith 1988a).

Perhaps the greatest issue related to WiggleWorks, and all such programs, is control. The old teaching paradigm implies that learning only happens when the teacher puts information into children's heads. The new paradigm implies that children can construct and learn about written language when they are in control. The new paradigm does *not* imply that the teacher is unnecessary. Indeed, a knowledgeable teacher who acts as a guide, facilitator, or fellow learner, is essential. Such a teacher *shares* control with learners during literacy acquisition. Obviously, putting a child alone in a room with the computer (discovery learning in its purest sense) is not going to work. Many children would walk out of the room the first time the computer failed to talk. There needs to be a teacher—better trained than before—to coach, consult, advise, offer suggestions, and most important, to nudge learners along as they expand their own personal written language. This requires a terrific amount of knowledge about how learning occurs. The new educator will have to have skills to pick and choose the strongest features from WiggleWorks and set up a literacy lab in the classroom. The teacher must recognize that students can be learning all day, not just during the time called, instruction. Instruction goes on all day, and it comes from the teacher, peers, and from the computer reading back a story. Most of all, instruction comes from within learners themselves as they risk, make errors, and teach themselves ways to solve problems.

WiggleWorks has many of the components needed in a literacy tool in the elementary classroom. It must be used by educators trained in how children are empowered by technology in acquiring written language. These educators must act as facilitators and coaches during this process. Scholastic is to be commended for its commitment to early literacy over the past 14 years, its incorporation of expert educational advisors of the caliber of Dr. Pinnell and Dr. Snowball, and its consultation with classroom teachers. Early research using this program with young children, although not nearly as extensive as IBM's research and commitment to Writing to Read, is very promising. Used appropriately and supplemented by an expanded talking word processor that allows extensive writing, WiggleWorks can provide a great start to the technology-based early interventions that should now be part of every classroom. WiggleWorks certainly should be reviewed by educators as they design early literacy environments.

SABES and SESOS Technology
for Second Language Learners

Dr. Maria Gonzalez-Baker is a renowned educator who has worked for 28 years as a bilingual specialist, researcher, and advocate for children in poverty who are learning a second language. She has devoted her career to improving the opportunities for success and learning of underprivileged learners of Hispanic culture. Recognizing the potential for learning that can be provided by computers, and dedicated to the belief that children in poverty should not be deprived of the finest learning opportunities education can offer, she designed computer software that could accelerate the development of cognitive academic language and the initial literacy skills of bilingual students and Spanish-dominant students. With the help of her brother, Peter Gonzalez, and cousin, Alfonso Gonzalez, she developed the first bilingual talking software—SABES (a tool to support a whole language approach to writing and reading in Spanish) and SESOS (an integrated language and science program in Spanish and English) (Gonzalez-Baker 1986).

Thanks to Gonzalez-Baker and her family, thousands of Spanish-speaking children in kindergarten, first- and second-grade classrooms have been afforded an opportunity to develop the fundamental literacy skills and the academic vocabulary to use in an academic setting and to launch them into the computer age.

The Southmost Elementary School Story

For a decade, Gonzalez-Baker collected writing samples in two languages and continually reviewed data that hundreds of teachers using SABES and SESOS provided her. The Southmost Elementary school in Brownsville, Texas, was a site located in the Southmost neighborhood and served 690 students. Ninety percent of the students came from homes where Spanish was the primary language and family income was well below the poverty level. A growing number of students and their parents were recent immigrants from Mexico. A significant number were also members of migrant families.

Gonzalez-Baker was invited to the campus by a new principal, Dr. Guadulpe Arevalo, to assist with curriculum development and teacher training. She was also asked to explore ideas regarding the use of technology programs in a bilingual setting and to discuss other areas of campus improvement. Arevalo is an advocate for children and an expert in the field of bilingual education. During their first meeting, he explained that the climate of the school needed to change. He described many of the barriers that existed on the campus. He was particularly distressed with the status of the bilingual program, the fragmented curriculum, the school climate, and the improper use of computers in the bilingual setting.

Soon after working with SABES and SESOS, Southmost Elementary teachers in grades K–2 became very proud of their students' improved results. They now refer to their students as *autorcitos* (little authors). Educators are pleasantly astonished at the quality and quantity of writing the students produce. Students read their own writings and approach books with greater confidence. The success at Southmost is directly related to the fact that the software is authentic, that is, it was custom designed for Hispanic students. It was not translation or adaptation of an English program.

A key factor in the program's success is its valuing of the childrens' first language (L1). Valuing the first language enhances the learning of the second language (L2). Negative attitudes about other languages, or belief that native languages interfere with English development, create anxiety, reduce self-esteem, and impair children's ability to learn. For both first and second language acquisition, comprehension is the key to development. Students need megadoses of comprehensible input in the early stages of language learning. During the early stages of language emergence, teachers should avoid correction of errors. Research has proven that correcting errors does not keep children from making mistakes. Rather, such correction produces anxiety about the new language (Krashen 1985). Likewise, teachers should avoid giving students grammar lessons in the early phases of L2 development. Exercises and drills do not help students learn a language any faster. The best learning occurs when there is no deliberate attempt to focus on the language itself. It is more important to focus on the functional aspects of communication than on grammatical structures. The computer opens up the world of communications to the student and is an excellent road to literacy in many languages.

The La Feria Story

Following is another success story, this one focusing on the use of SABES in Texas. Dr. Maria Gonzalez-Baker contributed this section.

The SABES Bilingual Program: La Feria ISD Incorporates Best Practices for Teaching and Learning in Two Languages with Talking Computers

La Feria, Texas is a small town located in the Rio Grande Valley just eight miles from the Mexican border. The town is surrounded by citrus orchards, vegetable farms, and cotton fields. In La Feria, 2,035 of the students attending public schools are of Mexican descent and 280 are Anglo Americans. For most students, Spanish is the dominant language. Many of the families in this community still live in poverty and depend on the extremely low wages earned doing seasonal farm work.

The majority of the children in La Feria do not speak English when they enter school—particularly in grades PreK–2. Furthermore, most fail to acquire the English language fast enough to meet the demands of academic instruction in an all English program. Because early failure in school destroys their self-confidence and leads many students to drop out before they reach the eighth grade, the primary goal of the La Feria School District since 1985 has been to invest in the development of its bilingual early childhood program. By emphasizing positive early learning experiences, La Feria expects to avoid expenditures on remediation of basic skills in the higher grade levels.

The program in La Feria was designed to operate on the positive assumption that the natural and effective development of Spanish and English bilinguals involves learning processes that are interrelated and make the languages interdependent. By holding to the hypothesis of the interdependence of Spanish and English, teachers were able to plan an instructional program that reflects pride in the home language and allows students to reach a threshold level of language and literacy development in both languages in order to meet the demands of the regular academic program in English more successfully once they exit the bilingual program.

The philosophy of the bilingual program in La Feria was one of "additive bilingualism." An "additive" bilingual program is based on the following tenets:

1. The program must operate within a school climate that respects the child's cultural heritage and involves parents in the learning process;

2. Teachers must utilize teaching strategies that reflect high expectations for achievement; encourage higher-order thinking and problem-solving skills; and promote self-esteem (examples: whole language, experiential and cooperative learning, process writing, shared reading, peer and cross-age tutoring); and

3. The program must allow ample time to reach optimum levels of proficiency in both languages.

Students in kindergarten and first grade received approximately 150 minutes of language arts instruction every day. Computers were an integral part of the whole language program, starting in kindergarten. Students each spent one hour daily in the

Spanish Acquisition Builds English System (SABES) Laboratory. The SABES program is based on a teaching methodology for Spanish literacy called Sistema de Escri-Lectura designed by Dr. Maria Gonzalez-Baker. Dr. Maria Gonzalez-Baker is a well known leader in bilingual education. She has received honors and recognitions for her outstanding, scholarly work by the Carnegie Foundation, the U.S. Department of Education, the Texas Education Agency, and the Mexican government. The SABES program she developed is a natural, whole language, high-tech writing program. The role of the computer is that of a powerful tool which facilitates the development of talking–writing and reading skills in Spanish. The role of the teacher is to guide the students to use multimedia tools to gain insights and skills for creative expression in their stronger language. The program outcomes at La Feria have consistently shown great progress. Parent involvement began to increase and teachers reported increases in attendance. Students began to appear more motivated to learn and seemed to enjoy writing and reading a great deal more than they had in the past—before they had computers. Teachers kept portfolios of students writings in both languages. Students in the SABES Program were writing longer stories, using more complex vocabulary than the students in the control program.

Dr. Gonzalez-Baker researched studies of schools using technology with ESL students. Below is a summary of what she discovered.

Studies on Using Technology with ESL Students

The Educational Testing Service of Princeton, New Jersey, was commissioned by IBM to conduct an extensive two-year evaluation of Writing to Read with more than 10,000 students in 21 sites. The study involved statistical comparisons of Basic Populations, which are more typically representative of the general school populations in the kindergarten and first grade across the United States. The study also involved comparisons of Special Populations, which targeted low-income and high-minority populations, including ESL students. The findings of the ETS Study were released in July 1984. Writing to Read students performed equally well, regardless of minority or economic status.

Houston, Texas, and Oakland, California, Results

The Oakland Unified School District in Oakland, California, and the Houston Independent School District in Houston, Texas, were among those who participated in the two-year National Demonstration Project of Writing to Read. Both of these urban school districts are highly diversified in their student populations with significant numbers of Black, Asian, and Hispanic children. Test results indicated that each of these groups performed at the same level equally well.

Washington, D.C., Schools Writing to Read Study Report

Many of the school districts involved in the original ETS study have extended their implementations of Writing to Read to other sites and continue to conduct their own investigations. Some are beginning to examine the effects of Writing to Read with non-English speaking children. Schools like Martin Luther King, Jr., in Washington, D.C., and Thompson Elementary School, on the edge of Washington's Chinese community, reported that non-English speaking children were scoring just as well as English speaking children across the city.

Red Mesa and Round Rock, Arizona, Schools

The Red Mesa Unified School District on the Navajo Reservation in Arizona received funds after submitting a proposal to the Johnson O'Malley Federal Office for Indian Education. They began implementation of Writing to Read during the 1984–85 school year with Native American children in grades K–4. Writing to Read was chosen to help enrich the language environment for the population where English is a second language. The first year results of students in Writing to Read were obtained from teacher interviews and questionnaires, student criterion referenced test scores, and observations. The report concluded that Writing to Read was highly successful. Significant improvements were noted in reading and writing performance for students in grades K–2. The evaluation study revealed that, although Writing to Read offered systematized and formalized writing for students in grades 3-4, the total program was not as effective for use with the older students. These findings are consistent with design of Writing to Read.

Kingsville, Texas

In 1984–85, the Kingsville Independent School District in Kingsville, Texas, received a Title VII grant from the U.S. Department of Education to investigate the effects of microcomputers in an early childhood bilingual setting. After a rigorous review of existing computer-based programs and a thorough investigation of the current research and literature, criteria were established for selection of a computer-based system which could best meet conditions for second language acquisition. Kingsville selected Writing to Read to accomplish the objectives for the English as a second language instruction of Spanish-speaking children in kindergarten through second grade. These students were participating in the school district's bilingual education program.

Teachers in the Kingsville Title VII Program reviewed developmental learning theories and second language acquisition theories. Every effort was made to incorporate natural second language development activities consistent with these theories with the activities prescribed in Writing to Read. Teachers reported that the "risk-free" environment, the high expectations, and the multisensory learning opportunities, which are integral aspects of Writing to Read are also very essential aspects of second language acquisition. The children in the Kingsville, Texas, schools responded very favorably to this approach to English language development. They began making the transition to English reading and writing very naturally and with remarkable speed.

Reports of the effectiveness of Writing to Read with ESL children in Kingsville, Texas, has prompted many other schools in Texas to adopt Writing to Read for use with ESL populations in kindergarten, first, and second grades. Teachers and parents of students participating in these new sites continue to report that ESL children are demonstrating similar results.

What to Do for Non-English Speaking Children

Donald Graves advises teachers to make sure non-English speaking children do not feel alienated from the rest of the class. He suggests that some procedures to help ESL children use English and feel at home are to choose mentors, or particular students in the class, to help them. Use pictionaries (or dictionaries with pictures) and many pictures and visual materials. Allow children to write on the computer, using their first language to get a sense of the transition they will make.

Research shows that handwriting and spelling are linked. When children write with an unpredictable scrawl, they get a poor visual image of the word, which hinders their spelling. If the child can work on a computer, the machine text not only adds prestige to the work, it enhances spelling as well (Graves 1994).

In kindergarten and first grade are the opportune times for the children to learn both languages naturally. It is not uncommon for children of these ages to mix languages in their writings, just as beginning learners of a language mix languages in early efforts. With encouragement and praise, the computer greatly enhances first and second language acquisition because it provides a visual picture of words; it allows students to decode new words by typing them into the computer and hearing them spoken; and it gives students access to a visual of the concept being learned, sounds of the language, and an ability to practice the language. Computer programs with speech recognition allow students to record their pronunciation of the new language.

It is a mistake to withhold the learning of English as a second language until sixth, fifth, fourth, or third grade, because language acquisition is a natural process for young children. The human brain is best at language acquisition between birth and age seven. Each child is an individual who constructs both the first and second language at his or her own pace. Young children acquire language naturally; therefore, their environment at school for learning and acquiring the second language should be acquisition-rich (Dulay and Burt 1973). For optimum bilingual language learning, schools need to teach children more than one language in preschool and primary grades, no later.

The computer is a tool for providing a great deal of comprehensible input or an acquisition-rich environment for the second language learner as well as an opportunity to continue learning concepts in the first language. *Bilingual and ESL Classrooms* suggests that if acquisition is an extremely important part of the acquiring-learning process, then teachers need to find ways to create more acquisition-rich classrooms for all ages. We must provide an appropriate balance of both acquisition and formal learning for older learners as well (Ovando and Collier 1985). Technology can help teachers provide an environment that provides this balance. In European schools, children learn up to five languages with little difficulty. The languages are introduced at early ages.

Parents understand the importance of an early start in bilingual education. Parents in Las Familia del Pueblo School (Los Angeles) attended a standing-room-only meeting to protest the school's bilingual program, which withheld English reading until fourth grade. Only 1 percent of the students mastered enough English to test out of the school's special bilingual classes (Pyle 1996).

Summary

Gonzalez–Baker's work points out the importance of valuing the first language of non-English speakers. Through SABES and SESOS, children learn to read English and Spanish in the primary grades, and they develop the Cognitive Academic Language needed in their native language. The technology empowers students and gives them the tools to be successful.

Adult Literacy

A middle-aged man waves to his friend across the street. "I'm going for my computer lesson now," he shouts as he enters the public library. In fact, he is learning basic reading skills with a tutor; in his mind, however, he is learning a modern skill that will help him retrain for the changing job market (Turkle 1984). Computers offer adult learners a new way to learn, a way that was not available to them as children.

Sherry Howie, in her chapter on adult literacy in a multiliterate society states, "Just as in the Paedrus, Plato feared that the invention of the paper and pen to record ideas would destroy the oral literacy tradition, writers such as Neil Postman (1992) fear that the inventions of television and computers will destroy our print literacy tradition. Whereas we were once a preliterate society, the invention of the printing press brought us primary literacy and the availability of the computer is turning us into a multiliterate society, one in which we learn and take in information in many different ways" (Radencich 1994). Computers used as language processors can be of tremendous benefit in the learning of language processing in reading and writing.

For adults who are illiterate or semiliterate, the use of computers for beginning instruction has many advantages. First of all, adult or high-risk high-school learners may have experienced repeated failure in traditional paper-and-pencil school tasks. Their problems may be directly attributed to eye–hand coordination. The ease of use of the keyboard, the association with the computer as a new way to learn and be successful, and computer use as a marketable tool, all make beginning literacy instruction on the computer a wise choice. Most adults find using the computer a matter of prestige and a boost to their esteem and confidence.

Another advantage to the computer is its multisensory presentation. Visual, auditory, and kinesthetic modalities are all involved in writing your own experience story and then listening to the computer read it back. The writer can listen to sections of the writing as often as necessary; this readily available feedback is vital to the learning process. The ease of editing on the word processor frees the learner from paper and pencil, erasers, correction fluid, and all the other methods of correction associated with writing things over until they are perfect. Possibly the greatest advantage of the computer is the collaboration with peers and the social skills it engenders.

IBM's Principles in Alphabet Literacy Program (PALS) showed just this capacity for engendering collegiality and successful literacy development. From the *Los Angeles Times* building in downtown Los Angeles, where *Times* employees visited the PALS lab one hour a day to improve their literacy skills, to the prisons of Ohio, which required prisoners to complete a 20-week literacy program on the computer as a condition of parole, PALS has been effective in improving adult literacy.

According to Jonathan Kozol, 25 million American adults cannot read the poison warnings on a can of pesticide, a letter from their child's teacher, or the front page of a daily newspaper. An additional 35 million read at a level lower than what is needed to survive in our society. "One out of every three adult Americans cannot read this book" (Kozol 1985).

To meet the needs of these 60 million people, representing one third of the entire U.S. population, a massive effort is needed. Technology offers great assistance and needs to be used throughout the country to help illiterate individuals.

One of the most significant features of using computers in adult literacy programs is the sense of empowerment they provide. The adult has control of his or her learning, and accomplishments become more meaningful. By accepting responsibility for educating themselves and controlling the pace and level of program accomplishment, adults become empowered to succeed. Learning computer skills also brings the adult learner into the world. Adults weak in literacy are denied access to so much of the world, they may be anxious about computers. Once they experience the ease of using a computer, they are eager and highly motivated to continue learning. Furthermore, computer know-how provides opportunities. These features and benefits are the same for all learners—adults as well as young children.

Computer instruction can be of many kinds. Just as in the children's area educators must carefully select appropriate software that puts the child in control of learning, they must do so or adults. The bottom-up approach to reading and skill drill software is as inappropriate for adults as it is for children. An electronic workbook or drill-and-kill program is equally ineffective, regardless of age. They are especially ineffective for adults who have already failed at this style of learning. Instruction that focuses on isolated skills taught out of meaningful contexts may not only frustrate adult learners but reinforce erroneous beliefs that reading is solely the ability to sound out words, rather than a meaning-making process (Radencich 1994).

IBM's Principles of Alphabet Literacy System

One such program that stresses reading as construction of meaning and utilizes the powerful language experience approach for adults was created the late 1980s.

The Principle of the Alphabet Literacy System (PALS) is a multisensory, self-paced writing and reading program that uses the advanced technology of interactive IBM multimedia systems to teach illiterate adolescents and adults to read and write. The PALS system was developed by Martin, a renowned educator for 35 years. It is designed to teach adolescents and adults who are below the sixth-grade level the following: writing, reading, touch typing, computer keyboarding skills, and word processing skills. It uses phonemic spelling to support the principle that students can write anything they can say. Students with very poor speech may be able to enunciate more clearly through use of this program. The foundation of the PALS curriculum is built upon a number of schools of thought and theory. These include the developmental processes of language and writing skills, learning theory, computer and video disc technology, and research and observation of how learning can be improved. The multisensory aspect of the videos and computer technology access different parts of the brain that facilitate learning. This is a new way of learning for human beings who have suffered many years of failure using traditional approaches to education. The typing and word processing taught in the program are seen by the adults as a meaningful job-related skill, and writing their life stories is a real world experience that boosts their self-esteem and pride in their developing literacy.

The program is designed to take 20 weeks of intensive daily learning. In one group, 17 high-risk high-school students were on the verge of dropping out of high school. None of them were functionally literate. Their downcast eyes and stooped shoulders indicated their low self-esteem. In the computer lab they were shown a new way to learn that they had not previously failed at. They were taught computer skills that would help them get a job in the real world, they were treated with respect and encouragement. Their writings were shared and encouraged. At the end of 20 weeks they had made an average of three years growth in reading, and were all able to write their autobiography and fill out important forms. Writing their autobiography, and other daily writings about their lives, made the word processing component of the program its most powerful asset. They walked out of the program with heads held high and a new attitude toward learning.

Incorporating writing into an adult reading program capitalizes on the strong relationship between reading comprehension and written composition, while accessing adults' wealth of information, interest, and experience. By using word processing to integrate reading and writing, adults become adept with the new technology in a creative atmosphere.

The state of Ohio used this literacy program as a condition of parole for prisoners. Statistics showed that the majority of prisoners are illiterate. Literacy gave inmates a chance for success in the outside world that they had never had before.

The *Los Angeles Times* established a PALS literacy lab in downtown Los Angeles for its employees with literacy problems. Probably the biggest disadvantage to this program was its expensive laser disk technology, touch screen media all in addition to computers made its implementation costly so it was replaced with a CD-ROM version. IBM stopped producing the PALS program one year ago, at this time they are still selling product they have left but will produce no new programs. The *Los Angeles Times* has a mobile literacy lab that travels to places where the people are and has added a process writing package to their program that helps adults fine tune their mechanics of writing. Of all the lessons learned with PALS, Martin said it best: "to energize people, to give them the great Eureka, now I understand, I can read, I can write!" Future program developers need to piggyback onto the successful aspects of this program and to create one that can give massive support to all high-school and adult illiterates. Since many convicts are illiterate and were not able to function in society, a program like this as condition of parole can make a big difference in the rehabilitation of the prisoner.

Working with adults who have experienced years of failure in learning adds another component, that of a low self-esteem as an illiterate in our society. The computer has many advantages over traditional technologies in learning, thinking and problem solving and in helping the adult illiterate population for above all it bolsters their self-esteem. The professional looking print that a new learner produces is empowering regardless of age level and something the adult illiterate has never experienced before. People have different learning modalities, and a multisensory approach would benefit the majority of learners by meeting their learning strength. A word processor provides many excellent benefits over using paper and pencil or a typewriter. Writers are freed to concentrate on their composing, knowing that they may easily edit their ideas later. Language thus becomes usable, mutable, and dynamic to the adult learner (Howie 1994).

Case Study on Adult Literacy

Just as stories of young children's literacy experiences are important to our body of knowledge about how children learn, so too are the stories about the adult learners involved in adult literacy programs.

Arthur, an African American adult with cerebral palsy, learned to read and write at the age of 33. Arthur exhibited difficulty with fine motor skills and had no control of his right hand, but he had good control of his left. Arthur really wanted to learn to read and write. It was determined to teach him using a computer. Because of his relatively good control of his left hand, a standard keyboard was used. The microcomputer was equipped with a speech synthesizer. The educators working with Arthur believed that what works for children works for adults. Whole language activities support students in their use of all aspects of language. Students learn about reading and writing while listening. They learn about writing from reading, and they gain insights about reading from writing. Choice is an essential element for learning. Teachers are facilitators who support the learning of individual students.

The researchers reporting Arthur's story conclude that the availability of computer equipment for experimenting with language provides a great opportunity for the non-speaking person. They found that there was no packaged program that would have helped Arthur to learn to read and write. His level of literacy was obtained only through a holistic approach, much as all early learners obtain their literacy (Gipe et al 1993).

Martin talked of energizing adult learners who had failed, of showing them the way to write and read and to tell their life stories. Researchers in adult and special education literacy are discovering that the truths researchers in early childhood literacy have found apply equally well to adult and special populations (Smith 1988b).

Summary

In closing, there are great universal principles that help guide the creation of literacy programs at any age level. Whether the learners are adults or children, and regardless of socio-economic status, culture, or gender, all the learners need to be respected for the experience, culture, and language they bring to the classroom. Treated with dignity and empowered by technology, these learners must be shown how their intelligence and their written words admit them to the literacy club. We cannot separate literacy from experience, culture, and traditions.

Programs like ELC, SABES, and SESOS are literacy learning tools effective for all youngsters.

Chapter 8

Integration of Computers into the Classroom

"My dog ate my homework" is the legendary excuse for missing homework assignments. The child who uses technology is more apt to come up with, "My brother stuck his doughnut in the disk drive," or "The dog chewed the computer cord" to explain missing assignments.

In *Understanding Reading*, Frank Smith cautions educators about the use of computers. In *Microcomputers: A Promise or a Threat*, he warns us that if the computer was just to be used as a drill-and-kill machine, delivering repetitious skill exercises, or as a computer aided instruction (CAI) system that plots every child's progress robotically and spits out meaningless test scores, we would be better off without them. He concludes that, "There is no evidence that such computer programs have succeeded in making children literate, and no convincing theories that they could succeed. Such programs could rapidly give children a totally false idea of the purposes and possibilities of literacy" (Smith 1988b).

The Place of Computers in the Classroom

This does not mean that computers have no place in the literacy classroom. As word processors, computers have helped the youngest children to become writers by assisting them in the physical act of writing. The computer also helps young children in drafting, editing, and preparing clean and legible copies of their texts. When used in these and a variety of other practical ways—in simulations, games, design activities, communication links, drama, art, and music—computers seem to stimulate children to talk more, plan more, think more, and write and read more. The issue is not whether computers should be in the classroom, but how they should be used (Smith 1988b).

Most of today's K–12 classrooms are filled with students "who have spent the greater portion of their lives staring at tubes of one kind or another, television, Nintendo, MTV, and computers are for this generation the primary medium of cultural transmission. From the playpen to early adulthood, the 13-inch screen, not the printed page, offers the dominant learning environment" (Winner 1994).

Teachers must sort out the hype about technology, the programs without educational value, the electronic workbook pages. They have a responsibility to sort the wheat from the chaff, or the valuable application of technology to writing and reading from the materials hawked and promoted as vehemently as the workbooks and textbooks of print media. A good teacher chooses the software applications students use in their learning. Consulting the Software Clearing House on the World Wide Web is the first step in checking out the ratings on the latest software and CD-ROM programs available for classroom use (Lathrop 1995).

It is never to early to introduce children to computers and word processing. Not surprisingly, children in grades K–8 already know much about computers. Children coming to school today have knowledge and experience with digital machines, from dishwashers to video game machines. It is the job of the teachers to select appropriate word processing and graphic tools and to guide children as they use these tools to enhance learning (Heller 1991).

The original practice of placing computers in a computer lab, where students visited for one hour a week, was a very poor beginning of computing into the school. This practice undermined the most valuable aspect of the computer—its ability to cut across traditional subject boundaries as a practical and useful tool. This lab approach minimizes the impact computers can have on children's learning by turning the technology into a separate, unrelated subject area called "computer literacy." Also, in this lab approach, students have access to about one-fiftieth of a computer in school, far from the critical level needed for this technology to have a major impact on learning experience (Papert 1993). Only when computers are integrated into the curriculum as a vital element for instruction and are applied to real problems for a real purpose will children gain the most valuable computer skill, the ability to use computers as natural tools for learning (Shade and Watson 1990).

Like any innovation, those of us who had to learn the hard way or old way sometimes have the feeling that, "We did it, so can they." We forget the number of learners who failed the old way and dropped out of school or literacy acquisition completely. Innovation requires a new way of learning. Old teaching practices need to be abandoned.

The talking word processor makes the physical task of writing easier. It is much easier to hit the a key to produce a professional looking A then try laboriously to create the letter with a pencil on triple-lined paper. But it is not just the manual job of writing that becomes easier for the learner. What has been written clearly on the screen gives the brain a clear visual image, and hearing the words spoken back provides auditory reinforcement. This auditory reinforcement is vital to auditory learners, and it helps all learners edit their work.

In addition, the whole onerous task of rewriting (and rewriting again) is made much simpler with the editing capabilities of the word processor. No longer must novice writers copy over the whole story again and again to correct the errors.

Finally, the best part of all, is printing the story. This provides proof the learner is indeed an author, a writer, a creator of a story worthy of being posted on the family refrigerator.

No classroom should be without computers. Ideally there should be one per child; in reality, there should be at least 6 computers per 30-child classroom to allow for daily access by each child. Children learn to write by writing and to read by reading, so they need to be able to write every day and to read their writing and their peers' writing as well as the good literature filling the shelves of the classroom. In *Mindstorms*, Seymour Papert suggests that each student should have his or her own powerful personal computer. Educators react to his idea with shock and amazement, declaring that finances make it impossible to purchase one computer per child. Papert points out that the direct public cost of schooling a child for 13 years, from kindergarten to twelfth grade, will be almost $30,000 by the year 2000. A high estimate of providing each child with a computer and of upgrading, repairing, and replacing it when necessary is about $1,000 per student, distributed over 13 years in school. Thus, costs for computers for the class of 2000 would represent only about 5 percent of the total public expenditure on education (Papert 1980). Papert is not alone in thinking that certain uses of powerful computational technology can provide children with new possibilities for learning, thinking, and growing emotionally as well as cognitively.

Not only is the hardware necessary, connectivity—connecting to global networks—is necessary, too. The Internet is the greatest resource of information ever to be made available to the classroom. In addition to providing information, it allows students to write meaningful messages, not only to others in their classroom, but to students all over the world. This is definitely a tool needed in every classroom.

Parents' Roles

Parents are a critical component in the early literacy development of their child. Their contribution is an essential element in their child's success as a writer and reader. Modeling writing and reading, reading to the child nightly, praising the child's early writings and reading as effusively as they praised early language development, and not correcting early approximations but always modeling correct writing and reading skills themselves. Taking the child on excursions to expand his or her background knowledge provides a good basis for early literacy. For parents who have computers in the home, providing early literacy programs, such as KidWorks 2, is a great help. Enthusiasm and interest in the child's learning, and patience in answering questions, are most important.

Creating an Enabling Environment

With computers in place, what students need most for literacy development is what Janet Emig calls an "enabling environment." According to Emig, this environment is "safe, structured, private, unobtrusive, and literate." She says that adults in this environment have two roles: "They are fellow practitioners and they are providers of possible content, experience and feedback" (Emig 1983). The place in which children learn needs to be supplied with resources and organized in ways that encourage independent learning. Time management is also critical. Children who are actively involved in teaching themselves need unbroken chunks of time in which to explore and test what they know (Karelitz 1993). Computers help teachers create the writing center environment they need to facilitate early writing development.

Teachers can turn their classrooms into exploratoriums, publishing centers, or research laboratories. Using software with which children discover concepts and cause–effect relationships, the computer provides a bridge between hands-on experiences and abstract learning. In such an environment children learn about a topic through exploration and experimentation (Papert 1993).

Respect for Children's Messages

The other most important ingredient for literacy success is adults who value and respect the messages and ideas children are trying to convey—adults who listen to the child, convey understanding of the child's message, communicate that understanding with a smile or a well-chosen response and encouragement. If adults constantly display amazement and delight at what children write, the children will write more and more and more.

All young children have an inner voice or intuition. (One five year old, asked "What does your daddy do?" responded matter of factly, "He lays on the couch and drinks beer.") Adults—parents and educators—must allow children to find their voice at age three and never stop writing and talking. Only by fostering their intellect do we allow them to become perceptive adults.

Funding for Classrooms

The National Assessment of Education Progress (NAEP) report on reading indicates that the reading scores in the state of Mississippi outshine those in the state of California (U.S. Department of Education 1995). This is amazing; historically, Mississippi has had one of the lowest literacy rates. How can the difference be explained? The governor of Mississippi, with funds from the Riordan Foundation, funded an IBM Writing to Read lab in all the first-grade classrooms in the state.

Why have the schools in the rest of the states been so slow to implement this idea? Cost is one reason. In California, the state provides $2.35 per pupil for technology, compared, for example, to Connecticut at $153.20, Kentucky at $149.15, Texas at $31.48, and Florida at $25.61.

Rapid obsolescence is another problem. Many schools established computer labs (full of Apple IIe machines) years ago, and the administrators and boards feel they have fulfilled the technology needs of the school. This is disingenuous. Any computer user knows a year or two is the longest you can use your computer without needing to upgrade or replace parts in order to run the latest software. Today's educational software is heads and shoulders above what was available 10 years ago. So administrators, boards of education, and teachers must plan for continual upgrading and acquisition of technology.

Innovative principals have "found" funds for technology by changing spending priorities. In addition, schools need help from business and industry to fund technology needs.

But hardware and software are not sufficient. "Humanware" is also required. Judging from the response to *Newsweek* magazine's second issue of Computers and the Family, a large number of parents of 18–24-month-old learners own computers and allow their toddlers to use them. Extensive studies like those reported by Dr. Rachel Cohen (see chapter 3) show that, on average, children can begin exploring the keyboard at three years of age (U.S. Department of Education 1995). Thus, a driving question is: When these learners come to school, will they find teachers who not only are competent technology users, but know how to encourage and facilitate computer-enhanced literacy growth.

Tips for Writing Success

All children have a story to write and are somewhere on the path of emerging literacy when they enter school. Teachers can help them on their journey by doing the following:

1. Accept the forms of writing and reading children use (Teale and Sulzby 1986).

2. Make requests simple: Write a story, write a letter to your mother, write some words you know.

3. Use reassurance, approval, and excitement. Reassure children they need not turn out perfect writing. Show that you understand the child's message and approve of the communication.

4. Let young students write daily. All young children have many stories to tell; you will get to know children from their writings.

5. Encourage expository writing. Graves suggests that every child has a topic on which they are an expert, or can become an expert. Inviting young children to study and write about a topic is a powerful way to involve them in literacy (Graves 1983).

6. Join Tele-Junior so students can communicate with students their age around the world. Letters written on computer and mailed—or better yet, telecommunicated—provide a sense of a global audience.

7. Use the computer during whole class and small group instruction and for recording class stories and producing class signs and charts.

Administrators are very important to the successful implementation of technology in the classroom. Their leadership and support is essential. Even the most visionary teachers cannot implement technology in the classroom if administrators lack vision and understanding of are unwilling to dedicate school funds to technology. It is vital that the vision of building a successful, integrated technology environment for students be shared by all elements of the community, the school board, administrators, teachers, staff, and parents. Teachers must attend conferences and workshops, take courses to update their knowledge, and read journals.

A Word of Caution

In no way do the authors imply that technology, in and of itself, is a panacea for school improvement or student learning. How computers are implemented in the classroom, how educators and parents model computer use, and adults' attitudes about the use of computers with young children are important to the success. Computers, whatever their enhancements, are learning tools—tools to use in thinking, writing, and solving problems. Like any sophisticated tool, the computer can be badly misused and when misused, it can be more of a hindrance than a help to learning. Figure 8.1 lists the "top 10" ways computers are misused in classrooms.

---

1. Limit use of the computer to reward students for completing drill worksheets.

2. Limit software to drill exercises or programmed learning exercises (that is, software that controls students).

3. Convey to students your own negative feelings about computers. Do not model the use of the computer for writing or reading.

4. Require students to write stories on lined manuscript paper, then copy them using the computer.

5. Insist that students' stories have perfect book spelling. If they do not, have a parent aide retype the stories to correct inventive spellings before the stories are printed.

6. Insist that students use only the teacher's chosen story idea or a list of words the teacher has provided. Don't let them indulge their own creativity.

7. Limit the time children can use the word processor to create their story to 15 minutes or less.

8. Do not allow children to print their daily writings, read them to the teacher and peers, or turn them into books to be taken home and read to parents.

9. Don't get excited about the writings children compose daily as they process language.

10. Don't ask for at least 6 networked computers in the classroom. Avoid training. Avoid using the computer for networking with colleagues, collaboration, and handling administrative tasks.

Figure 8.1 Ten ways teachers misuse computers

Suggested Ways to Use Computers in Integrated Curriculum

What is an integrated curriculum? True integration respects the interrelationships of the disciplines—language, mathematics, science—as natural and necessary to achieving the goal of becoming educated about a particular theme or topic of study. (Integrated curriculum is not an eclectic hodgepodge of materials that has no unifying theme or concept to explore.) Most themes to be studied evolve from students' interest and need to know (I-search rather than re-search).

When exploration of a concept includes writing reports, letters, stories, or poems, then using a word processor allows children to compose, revise, add, and remove text without being hampered by the tedium of forming letters or the messiness of crumbling erasures. Research shows that children who write on word processors compose longer and more complex stories, are less worried about mistakes, and are more willing to revise (Clements 1987).

The teacher doing a unit on the theme of Family could have the children use the KidWorks 2 software to construct pictures of their families, then add labels that can be narrated in each child's voice by recording through the computer's microphone. Each child then could make a presentation to the class. Also using KidWorks 2, each child could write and draw the story of his or her life and hear the composition read back. Or, the teacher could play a song about family for students, distribute copies of the lyrics, and suggest children write their own lyrics based on things they remember about their grandmother's house. Then they can sing their version of the song for the class.

The Teacher's Role in the Writing Process

One of the most important things a teacher can do in the classroom is to model reading, writing, speaking, loving literature, and using technology. Students want to be like successful adults. They will be motivated to use the computer no matter what, but they will be much more likely to use the computer as a practical, integrated tool for learning if they see a teacher doing the same.

Helpful strategies to use when students are writing with computers include:

1. Be friendly, patient, and encouraging.

2. Sit at the student's eye level.

3. Encourage the child to spell words the way they sound.

4. Keep the focus on the flow of ideas. Ask leading questions.

5. Ask questions to extend stories.

6. Give specific praise.

7. Provide opportunities to read and share stories.

8. Provide guidance in hearing phonemes.

9. Help the child edit for phonemic consistency.

10. Avoid writing as copying.

11. Guide self-editing.

12. Accept quiet talking.

13. Provide multiple materials and orderly storage.

14. Value students' writing by posting and publishing their works.

15. Augment the coaching staff with volunteers, older students, and peers.

The computer can never substitute the personal touch of the classroom teacher. In fact, even more skilled teachers are need to model, facilitate, coach, and instruct students in this new medium.

How to Implement Computers in the Classroom

How teachers implement computers is critical. Without proper integration of computers into the curriculum, the benefits of technology will not be attained.

Four to six networked computers are a good start for the classroom. (Networked means linked together so that all the software is loaded onto the system server and teachers do not have to handle disks.) Of course, if cost was no object, a computer for each student would certainly be ideal. Failing that, even one computer with a talking word processor is an asset to any classroom.

Let students create their own stories, poems, songs, plays, and journals. Be a facilitator, that is, encourage and nudge children to the next higher level. This requires you to have faith in young children and to recognize that each one desires to learn and succeed. If students appear unwilling to learn or if they have been labeled lazy, bad, dumb, or stupid, then something has gone wrong for them in their learning environment. See beyond the label, find the person, and lead him or her to a new tool, a new way to become an author. Introduce them to the talking computer, and let them experience the empowerment of the language machine.

In the past, teachers using the language experience approach, spent long hours copying dictated stories, unaware they were sending the student a subliminal message of failure. Now the balance of power has shifted, and the learner writes directly on the computer, without adult intervention. The first publication may be a simple one (i.e., I luv u dad n mum). But when printed out and illustrated, then proudly taken home to be displayed in the place of honor on the kitchen refrigerator, it becomes much more than a simple sentence. It is proof of membership in the literacy club.

The language machine makes authorship and book publication easy. After a teacher reads a book, such as *Charlotte's Web* (White 1952), to the class, students can go to the word processor and create stories told through the eyes of their favorite animal character. In fact, as students are introduced to classics and stories of all genres, they will be motivated to create stories of that type. One language arts program in a California school revolved around an invitation to Ray Bradbury to visit the school to talk about his writing. In preparation for his visit, the students read Bradbury's works, listened to readings of them, and then used language processing to create their own stories written in his style.

In one classroom, after reading Sendak's, *Where the Wild Things Are* (Sendak 1963), the teacher used the software Monsters and Make-Believe. The first graders became Max and created their own monsters in words and pictures. Each creation was given words carefully chosen by diligent first-grade authors, and 20 original big books were added to the classroom library to be read and re-read by the resident authors.

Creative teachers also realize that K–5 children need to read works of nonfiction and practice writing factual reports in preparation for content area readings in science and social studies. Language processing makes the creation of reports fun and easy, and listening to one another's reports a way to acquire needed writing and reading competency (Casey 1991).

How Do Children Do Language Processing?

After years of observing young children at the keyboard, I have recorded the process by which they achieve literacy when using the microcomputer as their learning tool.

Exploration. Initially, students explore the keyboard and type random letters. (This exploration is an essential learning stage. As children type, they see each letter, hear it, and are actively involved in the process of teaching the letters to themselves.) Alphabet recognition has been shown to be an indicator of reading success.

Encoding and copying known words. Next, students type their name and words familiar to them (like Mom, Dad, Ruff). They also look around for print; they type the print into the computer to hear it spoken and see its form. They continually search for meaning and patterns in the letters and words they create on the screen.

Writing explosion. Finally. students begin to put their own thoughts together with all these words. The extension from one sentence to long stories occurs very rapidly. At this stage, the learner needs to hear the teacher read many varied examples of good literature. The variety of styles and content serves as a font of ideas for children to assimilate, adapt, and use in the creation of their own individual stories.

Printing. The final proof of membership in the literacy club is the professional looking computer printout of their own writing. This is the proof that the writer is indeed a real author and a literate person.

Software for Language Processing

The place to begin when integrating technology in the classroom is to determine the goals you wish to accomplish, then find the software that achieves those goals and choose the hardware that will run those programs. Refer to the California Instructional Technology Clearinghouse for the latest reviews of software (Lathrop 1995).

Presently, the best software programs to use for language processing are Writing to Read 2000 coupled with Write Along, both from IBM, or KidWorks Deluxe and KidPhonics, both from Davidson. KidPhonics is a vast improvement on the phonics software in the original Writing to Read program and in other previous software. It includes music and song lyrics and allows the child to notice sounds in meaningful context. It is exactly what teachers have been asking for. But with the rapid technology explosion, newer better products are always on the horizon. Educators must continually review new software products that accomplish classroom goals.

Computers allow users to move easily between text and graphics. Most children use a combination of graphic forms and keyboard letters from early preschool into first grade. At first, they often type random letters and enjoy listening to the sounds the computer makes as it reads them back. Children find some strings of letters and words hilarious, and they often laugh out loud at the sounds they have created. When they hear the computer mispronounce a word, they find it amusing; but as they become more fluent they begin to change their spelling so the computer says the words the children want it to say.

Children adapt easily to computer writing. They start with hunt-and-peck. This helps them attend to alphabet recognition and also develop strategies they need to write. They definitely do not need touch typing to begin writing!

Through students' writings, teachers come to know students and the problems they face in their daily lives. In one class, a first-grade girl wrote an especially poignant story based on her own experience. Although this little girl chose a fictitious name and culture for the girl she wrote about, the problem in the story was her own. Her mom was pregnant but didn't tell her; in fact, the mom thought her daughter didn't know what the word *pregnant* meant! The child was feeling excluded and worried about sharing her parents' attention with a new baby. A teacher reading this kind of story can use discussion and reading of literature (like *Peter's Chair* by Ezra Jack Keats) to help the child work through her fears. Without children's daily, personal writing, the teacher could never provide this type of meaningful learning before.

Daniel, a five year old Hispanic student was focused and compelled to write as he wrote his own Spanish version of Disney's Lion King story and then set it to music for his whole class of five year olds to enjoy.

The word processor is a perfect companion to a literature program. Children's reading skills grow from daily rereading of their own writing, as well as from daily reading of literature books, their peers' writing, and (don't forget) the teacher's writing. Many children like to create their own versions of stories from books, and it is not unusual to see them bring a book to the computer to assure that they use a conventional spelling or idea.

Sam wrote the following story after hearing *Rosie's Walk* (Hutchins 1968) read out loud by the teacher. Sam adopted the style of a pattern story as used by the book's author. Notice Sam's use of humor in the last sentence of this story.

> A turtl   .   went across A pond.he   met a duck.   the duck   took a   walk
> with the turtl   then   they met a hen. The hen took a walk with the turtl and
> the duck. Then they   met a cat. then they went up a hill.   then they went
> down the hill. then they were lost.

Models of Implementation

Classroom Models

This section focuses on specific models of classroom use of networked computers to answer questions like: How many computers should be in each classroom and how should they be utilized? What do you do if you only have one computer? How can a teacher provide equal access to all students? What are some of the many ways teachers have effectively motivated students to become writers and readers using technology? How can teachers use telecommunications to collaborate with other teachers worldwide on Internet? How does Internet telecommunication create a meaningful writing environment for early literacy students?

Mary Zirm's Class

In Mary Zirm's first-grade classroom at Nightingale School in Orcutt Unified School District, Santa Maria, California, there are six networked computers in a technology corner. Students rotate daily through this center and write their own stories, journals, plays, thoughts, and reports. Then they have the opportunity to sign up to be author of the day and present their talking computer composition to the class on the overhead using the LCD projection monitor. Positive feedback is given to each author by peers. Sometimes students pair up to write a collaborative story and make a joint presentation.

Jenny McNiven's Class

In Atlanta, Georgia, Jenny McNiven's classroom is organized in learning centers. The kindergarten students who go to the telecommunications center write notes to their friends in Mark Burn's classroom in Alaska. They put copies of the notes they send and receive in a book, which they have bound with yarn and titled Our Alaskan Friends. This book resides in the book corner and is frayed from many little hands. Students enjoy reading it and talking about their Alaskan Internet classmates.

Cindy Clegg's Class

Cindy Clegg's first-grade classroom in Santa Barbara, California, is a warm, whole language, literature-based environment. Most of the students are bilingual. She uses both English and Spanish software in the computer learning centers. She has found that her students are learning both languages well at the same time.

Their early writings in their native language astound her. One student, Oscar, wrote a five-page story in Spanish, his first language. Oscar also is writing stories in class in English; however, starting out in his most fluent language has given him great confidence as he learns his second language. He is as successful at writing on the computer as anyone else in the class.

Some programs have kept second language learners out of the computer lab, thinking that such learners cannot use computers until they are ready to learn English—at some more advanced age. This Santa Barbara teacher shows how well early literacy can occur in both languages.

Jennifer Casey's Class

The students in Jennifer Casey's special education (first to fifth grade) class, in Prince William County, Virginia, have collaborated on a class book. Using the computer, the students have created a story about a dinosaur complete with illustrations. They printed it out as a big book and placed it in the reading corner. The students enjoy re-reading it to one another daily.

Model of Classroom Design

Each teacher must design the classroom based on its space and layout and the needs of the students. Following are some suggestions about what is needed to make each classroom a writing, publishing environment.

Set up the room in centers, or areas, for specific purposes. Include a library center with plenty of comfortable places to read. (Ask parents to donate some rocking chairs for this area.) An Author's Chair provides a place for authors to read their latest works. A computer center, with at least six networked computers, provides a place for budding writers to write across the curriculum all day long. A U-shaped coaching table allows you to talk with children about their writing and offer feedback and suggestions. An editing area provides a place for peer conferencing and collaboration, as well as editing. (Provide baseball caps labeled Editor for children working in this area.) A telecommunication center, where at least one computer is hooked to an online service, allows students to communicate daily with counterparts elsewhere in the world. A presentation center with hypermedia capability allows groups of children to develop plays, stories, reports, and presentations, then (using the projection monitor) share them with the entire class.

Don't forget a computer on your own desk and an LCD projection monitor so you can daily make presentations, share your writing, and edit your own work. You will find your computer to be invaluable for writing frequent parent notes, communicating with colleagues online, and for recordkeeping.

Model of Funding for Implementation

An Illinois School District provides a model of computer implementation throughout a district. Superintendent Dr. Mike Risen of the Midwest Central District 191 in Illinois went out on a limb to introduce technology into all of his classrooms. He knew the impact technology could make, and he was determined to provide Midwest Central's 1,350 students and teachers with the advantages of technology. Working with his staff he made budget trade-offs and allocations to provide money that was needed. As part of this process, he developed leadership teams of teachers and administrators.

Computers with such programs as Writing to Read; Writing to Write; and language arts, math, and science programs were first added in the kindergarten and primary grades. Computers and multimedia software were also added at the high school. Today, there are more than 300 PCs installed in the district's four schools. Technology in the classroom has resulted in a 30 percent increase in student scores on the Illinois Goal Assessment Program, according to Risen. He recently initiated a grant to replace teacher desktop workstations with laptop computers. Teacher training is ongoing; the district gives teachers the option of taking their computers home. This option has allowed teachers to enhance their skills to use the system for preparation of classroom materials. This innovative superintendent plans to make laptops available for every student in his district by the year 2000. This sort of vision, when it encompasses an entire educational community, can make technology happen.

Model of Online Access

Students in junior high and high school now have resources available at their fingertips, if their classrooms are connected to the Internet. A political science or government class no longer needs to be a boring place to spend an hour memorizing facts about the Constitution. Instead, through innovative programs found on the Web, such as CapWeb (http://www.policy.net) or the U.S. Senate (http://www.senate.gov) or House of Representatives (http://www.house.gov), students can get up-to-date information about the government, read about current issues, and write to senators and representatives (Casey 1996). Being involved in real-world issues, rather than debating questions in textbooks, can empower adolescents to take more interest in their government and the community.

In educational methodology, the pendulum continually swings. Innovations come and go. At first they are touted, but gradually they are replaced. Jaded educators may hold out, to see whether the interest in computers will wane. They will have a long wait, for this is an innovation capable of an impact as astounding as the telephone or the printing press. The language machine is not a passing fancy, any more than a pencil or pen is.

Model of Teacher Training

If you are a teacher who has never had the opportunity to use the computer, perhaps the best way to begin is to overcome fear of the technology. Purchasing a computer is a personal option that is well worth the expense. Go to a computer store and ask a salesperson to explain your options. Read computer magazines evaluations and ask knowledgeable friends to recommend hardware they have used and like. Start with good word-processing software, then add an online service like America Online. This will open up a world of information and put you in touch with other educators around the world. Many will be as new to this adventure as you are, so you will learn together. Most of all, try to recapture the fearlessness of learning that young children exhibit.

Summary

The computer and the ability it gives us to reflect on the information resident in our brains, as well as accessing the information that is resident in the billions of other brains, can open up a learning revolution like we have never known. Perhaps what we have learned most from our research with the language machine as we have tried to use it to empower human beings, is the immense power the human brain has to learn and to grow when given the right environment and allowed to pursue its own path.

There are many ways that the teacher can integrate technology into her classroom to make the job easier, to empower the writing of all students, to enrich curriculum and to bring to the classroom the resources of the world. The time to start is now, so that every child has a chance for literacy success and access to the information needed as a citizen of the twenty-first century.

Chapter 9

Technology Program Evaluation

Understanding learning from the student's point of view forces educators to examine their own ethnocentricities.

Taylor 1993

To find out whether an innovation enhances learning, we must ask the learners, observe them, look at their writings and listen to their words. Next, we must ask those closest to the learners, their parents and teachers. Finally, we might glance at the isolated reading test score results that measure answers to questions written under test-anxiety conditions. These test questions were written by some distant individual who has no knowledge or acquaintance with the learners who must answer them. For generations, educators have relied on this paltry quantitative evidence to measure learners because we have had nothing better. Standardized test scores alone yield results influenced by myriad factors beside the program being evaluated. Educators must demand better evidence of learning than these tests provide. The best evidence is the type used by the medical profession: Observation and reports from students. This type of evidence is gathered through extensive ethnographic observation and recording, self-report from those involved, and samples of the literacy products produced by those in the program.

Any program implemented in schools must be carefully thought out and designed to meet the needs of children. The ideal evaluation tool has not yet been invented, but after years of standardized testing, one thing is clear: A standardized test gives limited information. True, it can offer comparisons of how well various children respond to questions developed by a particular testmaker—at a single point in time. But in evaluating programs, more information than that is needed.

As long as educators are constrained by public demand and administrator dictum to scores of standardized tests, this quantitative information will be used in evaluating new programs. However, just as educators gather "single shot" data from standardized tests, so they must gather a great deal of qualitative data (information about how children are learning in this program and how teachers and parents feel about this learning) *over time*. A two-week testing session or quick walk through classes does not do it. A good evaluation takes a minimum of two years. The first year of an innovation is training, putting the innovation in place, and working the bugs out. It takes a second year to really observe what is happening with children's learning in a classroom.

A Recent Qualitative Evaluation

The Simi Star Project was a two-year project to examine implementation of computers in the kindergarten and first-grade classrooms of 24 classrooms in 6 school districts. The final report is reprinted here as an example of the qualitative evaluation studies that can be conducted by researchers and educators to provide a firm foundation about decisions pertaining to integration of technology in the curriculum.

Six school districts—Simi Valley, Orcutt, Oxnard, Hueneme, Santa Barbara, and Ventura—joined in a technology partnership with IBM in 1990. The first goal of this large-scale project was to demonstrate the use of a Writing to Read (WTR) adaptation that supports a literature-based, whole language, writing process environment in kindergarten and first-grade classrooms. The second goal was to enhance teacher productivity and competence. A comprehensive-teacher training model and telecommunications network was developed. Teachers attended several workshops and received on-site support and telecommunications coaching for implementation. The third goal addressed a serious physical plant problem facing many school districts: lack of space. Placing the technology equipment directly in the classroom eliminates the need for separate space for computer labs. Networking classroom computers provides freedom from disk swapping and allows young children to independently log on and use computers throughout the school day. This study compared WTR in the classroom with WTR in a lab setting and in settings without computers in the classroom. The questions the study asked were:

- Does integrating technology into the classroom become a natural extension of the teaching methodology and a familiar, nonthreatening tool available throughout the school day to students?
- How is the equity of use an important issue for the schools?
- How can a qualitative evaluation approach provide better data about the effect of computers in the classroom on students' writing and reading progress?

Writing to Read is a computer-based language arts program designed to foster literacy development (writing and reading) of young children. The computer is used to both individualize instruction, so that children can work at their own pace, and also to create a new classroom milieu in which computers are used for cooperative groups and writing collaboration. According to a recent report from the Center for the Study of Writing and Literacy, "Computers do not function as independent variables in classrooms, but rather as part of a complex network of social and pedagogical interactions" (Greenleaf 1992).

The issue is not whether computers can be used effectively. The issue is how they can be used. This study seeks to show how teachers can best take advantage of the power and flexibility of computers to enhance student learning in their classrooms.

The following evaluation was the first qualitative evaluation of the Writing to Read program in the classroom.

The Simi Star Evaluation Project

The evaluation of the Simi Star Project was led by Dr. Jean M. Casey, associate professor of reading/language arts, California State University, Long Beach; Ellen Lee, assistant superintendent of curriculum, Simi Valley School District; Sherrie Kolz, IBM education instructional specialist; 6 principals; and 36 teachers and coordinators in the school districts.

In order to determine the effectiveness of the WTR program in developing literacy skills of kindergarten and first-grade students, a two-group experimental design was employed. To ensure a valid comparison of the effects of the WTR program with current instructional practices, both the experimental and control groups were selected from the same school districts.

A qualitative evaluation plan, modeled after Dr. Casey's Descriptive Study of the ABC School District reading program and Dr. John Goodlad's national study of schools, was developed. Instruments for evaluation included: Observations in the classroom, pre- and post-reading attitude surveys, year-long portfolios of writing samples, teacher questionnaires, parent questionnaires, administrator interview and questionnaires, student interviews, and teacher and administrator journals. Qualitative data was compiled in anecdotal record form. Results from interviews, questionnaires, and journal reports were presented in percentages. One thousand writing samples were scored using a holistic rubric scale.

[A timeline for this appears in figure 9.1.]

Training

Training was a vital part of this project. Lack of sufficient training is one of the biggest areas of failure in the implementation of technology in the schools.

Major Conclusions

Conclusion 1: The most successful results occurred in school sites where the desire for the integration of technology in the classroom originated with the classroom teachers and the site administrator shared their interest and desire to participate in this program. The elements of teacher and administrator expectation, enthusiasm, and interest and support for a program are vital elements in the success of any school innovation.

Conclusion 2: Over 1,000 writing portfolios were collected from K–12 students representing 29 classrooms in 6 school districts. Included in the population were several Spanish-language classrooms, ESL classrooms, and classrooms with learning handicapped students.

All students in the experimental Writing to Read in the Classroom program averaged at least two writing levels higher then those in the control classrooms. The experimental group had a significantly higher positive reading attitude than the control group. All students were included in the study. Those identified as ESL, LD, ADD, or gifted achieved the same benefits from the program as did other students. Equity of technology use was provided for all.

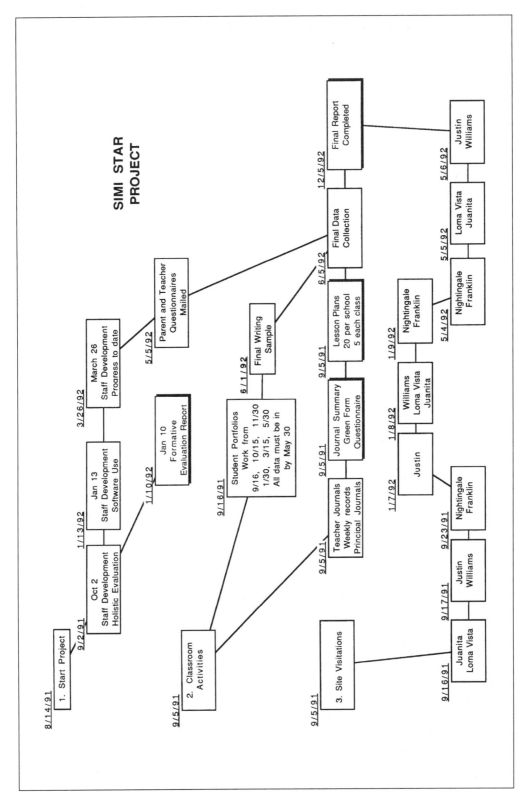

Figure 9.1   Project timeline

The Criteria for Scoring Writing Samples was based on an adapted version of the holistic rubric used by Educational Testing Service in the national WTR evaluation. It covers eight levels of scoring for writing samples, starting with blank, pre-writing, and six levels of writing proficiency, with descriptions of benchmarks for each level. Teachers were trained in the use of holistic scoring. Samples were gathered from the experimental group of writings done with pencil as well as on the computer. The control group, since it had no computer access, responded by pencil only. (See appendix A for Holistic Scoring criteria.)

[Figures 9.2–9.4 show statistical results.]

Questions Frequently Asked by Superintendents, Principals, Teachers, and Parents

How valid is holistic scoring and qualitative research? Holistic scoring has been used by the State of California in the CAP test since 1985. National assessment reports encourage educators to use this type assessment. In a qualitative study such as this, we were able to measure writing growth through assessing 1,000 writing portfolios using a holistic rubric for scoring writing samples. We also were able to measure attitudes and behavior through questionnaires and observations. The elements of empowerment and student self-esteem that are an important part of computer integration have been missed by prior research that focused on standardized test reading scores alone. Positive reading attitudes, as well as double the amount of writing growth, was uncovered and validated in this benchmark study. Future studies such as this one should be conducted in our school settings to measure, describe, and validate implementation of technology in the classroom.

When will my child transition to book spelling? The average Writing to Read first grader had improved four levels of writing proficiency, bringing most of them into [the] transition to book spelling.

What do parents think of this program? Parents in the WTR experimental classrooms gave a 95-percent rating of how much they liked the program and their children liked it. They gave a 99-percent rating on knowing about how this program taught their child reading and writing. In the control groups over 50 percent of parents had no idea what program of reading or writing was being used in the classroom.

Parents in the WTR samples reported significantly higher evidence of writing and reading behaviors their child demonstrated at home than parents in the control group. Twice as many students in the WTR program wrote stories at home, and three times as many WTR students wrote notes at home, so both observable reading and writing behavior were significantly enhanced. Actual changed literacy behavior in the home environment is a much more powerful indicator of literacy development than a score on a standardized test. Educators should include ongoing parent evaluation of their child's literacy growth in the home environment.

Of course this works for the average child, but my child is said to have attention deficit disorder. How can it help him? Experimental classrooms with ADD children reported they were doing high-level writing due to the ease of use of computer as opposed to the struggle of using a pencil, and had a positive attention span during their time on

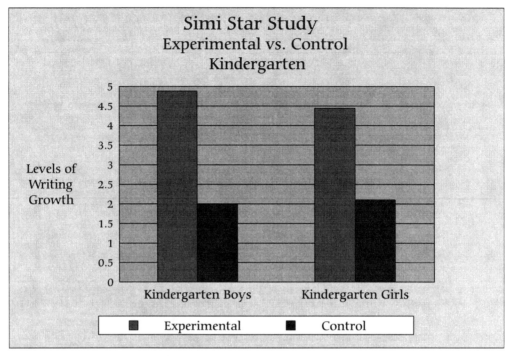

Figure 9.2   Results of kindergarten writing, experimental group versus control group and boys versus girls

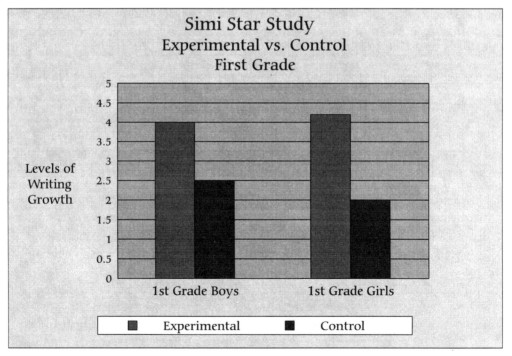

Figure 9.3   Results of first-grade writing, experimental group versus control group and boys versus girls

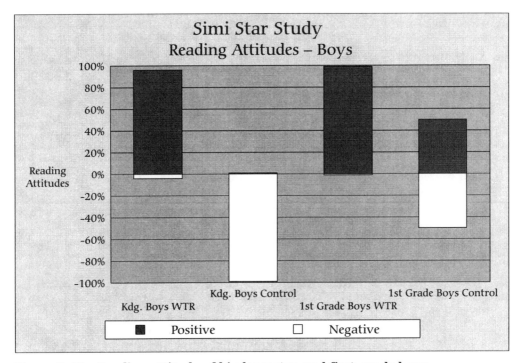

Figure 9.4A   Reading attitude of kindergarten and first-grade boys

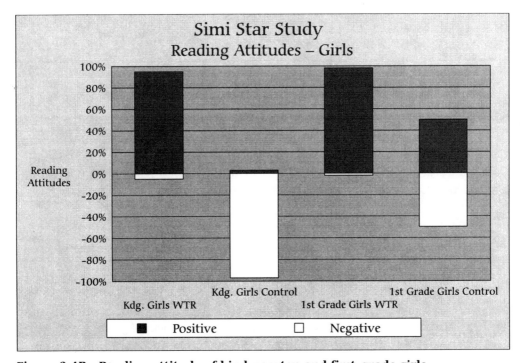

Figure 9.4B   Reading attitude of kindergarten and first-grade girls

the computer. Computer use seems to be a highly successful intervention for students labeled ADD, dyslexic, and other learning disorders. Further research needs to be conducted specifically on the effect of computers for empowering these learners.

My child is learning English as a second language. How can it help her? The Spanish experimental classrooms had many striking examples of ESL students empowered by computer use. One fourth-grade student non-English speaker from Mexico learned English well enough in six months to become the computer monitor in his fourth-grade class. The principal reported that this boy turned from a high-risk student to a leader in the fourth grade due to this computer program in the classroom.

What do teachers think of Writing to Read in the Classroom with Stories and More multimedia software? The combined experience of the teachers involved in the experimental study was 438 years, or an average of 18 years per teacher. Teachers rated the overall program 4.14 on a 5 point scale, with 4 being liked it and 5 being liked it very much. Teachers reported they felt that this program improved the students writing and reading significantly and reported they had now made computers an integral part of their classroom. One teacher summed up all of their feelings perfectly when she said, "How terrible it would be to be forced to go back to teaching without computers!"

What did principals think of this program? Principals reported 75–100 percent integration of computers in all K–1 classrooms. They felt the most positive results were for their students and their teachers in providing a risk-free environment for learning within classrooms. They were proud of the success they saw for both students and teachers. They also found that the parents were really pleased with their child's use of technology and the reading and writing their child did at home and at school.

How did Writing to Read in the Classroom compare with WTR in a lab and the control classrooms with no computers or WTR? Boys and girls in the Writing to Read in the Classroom experimental groups were writing at higher levels than the boys and girls in the WTR lab or control groups. However, the WTR lab students wrote at higher levels than the traditional classroom control group. [See figure 9.5.]

Additional Findings

The use of networking computers in the classroom was found to be extremely effective by teachers, once the networks and computers were finally up and running. (Do not underestimate the time it takes to make this a reality.) This entire project was delayed a full year due to the difficulty with obtaining, assembling, and troubleshooting equipment and facilities—and this was when the equipment was all free. Sites seeking to replicate this type of program will want to include sufficient time for equipment installation and then schedule training after all equipment is up and running. Short-changing equipment installation and teacher training will lead to an unsuccessful program. Networks allow teachers access to many software programs without having to load and unload disks; they allow teachers to choose other software based on their needs, their students needs and interests and have the system operator install it on the network. Teachers can design classes that contain software packages they choose for specific groups of learners. Networks greatly decrease the workload in the classroom, so where Writing to Read labs with standalone software required an aide just to load cycle software, now kindergarten and first-grade students can access their software

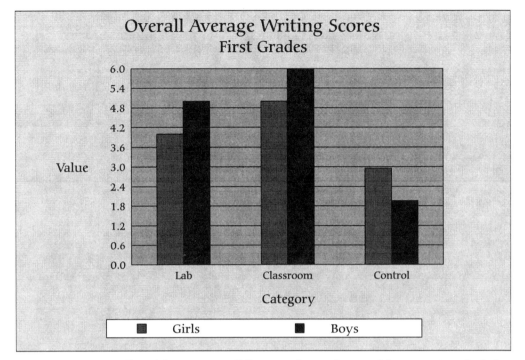

Figure 9.5   Overall writing scores of first-grade students with computers in lab, computers in classroom, or no computers

alone with great ease, and this additional support is not needed. In fact although additional aides, parent volunteers are important parts of the literacy classroom, once children and teachers are comfortable with the computers and networks the program can be effectively used by the one teacher classroom, cross-age tutors from middle grades are the perfect additional tutors to use in this type classroom.

The level of knowledge of technology use among the teachers and their integration of technology into their curriculum and classroom day was probably one of the most positive results of the study. When asked if they would continue this program the following year after completion of the study and without any further outside support, the teachers reported a 100-percent response that they would continue the program and would no longer want to work in a classroom without computers as a vital part of the learning environment.

The tapes of literature books and the literature books selections included in the Writing to Read program were found to be very effective by all teachers. They rapidly included Spanish tapes and books and their own tapes and books at this station, yet they all concurred that the vital auditory reinforcement provided by students listening to books on tape and reading along with them was a valuable literacy experience in the classroom.

Beyond the phenomenal growth in writing for all the students who had computers available in the classroom, the over-1,000 samples of children's writings yielded valuable documentation and evidence of the children's metacognitive awareness about the conventions of writing, they showed it in the developmental patterns of their daily written work. When a printed story showed words all clustered together like Sean's, who wrote retofthejedi (Return of the Jedi) as if it were one word, and evidenced his lack of awareness of space between words. With daily reading of literature books, Sean made the observation of how space between words helped the reader, and his next computer writing sample had large spaces between each word. Some samples had many periods or punctuation marks on the page, a clear sign that in experimenting with language and writing, the author had just discovered periods and question marks. The daily computer writing samples are fantastic evaluations of not only what the child is interested in, thinking about, but also his present mastery of syntax, punctuation, and spelling. These samples, when saved in a portfolio, are wonderful authentic assessment tools for parents, the child, and the teacher to confer about and witness progress.

One experimental K/1 classroom reported Attention Deficit Disorder (ADD) children and one dyslexic. They were all doing good writing on the computer and were not discernible to observers as being learning disabled. The teacher reported this as one of the most difficult classes she had ever had behaviorally and yet easiest to manage and most successful in writing when involved on the computers with WTR in the classroom.

Teachers and principals in experimental groups reported wanting to continue the program the next year and feelings that it was extremely successful with all their students but particularly, ESL, LEP, ADD, LH, and gifted students.

The results clearly showed that:

1. The most successful results occurred in school sites where the desire for the integration of technology in the classroom originated with the classroom teachers and the site administrator shared their interest and desire to participate in this program.

2. School sites in which there was interest in the project by only some of the classroom teachers and the site administrators produced the next best results, but only in the classrooms of the staff interested and supportive of the project.

3. School sites in which there was dissension between the site administrator and the teachers, year-round school implementation, lack of teacher interest or administrator interest (in one case the administrator was removed and another replaced and given the program without any interest or buy in) were the least successful.

The element of teacher and administrator expectation, enthusiasm and interest and support for a program are vital elements in the success of any school innovation.

Program Strengths and Weakness

Based on results of classroom observations and reports by teachers and principals in journals and interviews, the following recommendations were made.

- Teachers unanimously supported the use of Stories and More, a multimedia-based software, as an outstanding support to their current literature programs and a motivator for student writing and reading. This program supports all the goals of the California State Framework and was found to be effective with both kindergarten and first-grade students. The second element of the program they felt was most important was the word processing functions available to the students on Primary Editor Plus and Children's Writing and Publishing software. Teachers discovered that the students in both kindergarten and first grade can benefit from using the word processor from the first week of school. They discovered the fact that written development on the keyboard does occur in stages akin to the stages of language development. They also observed and discovered that many 5–7 year olds do not yet have sufficiently developed eye–hand coordination to successfully print their thoughts and ideas with a pencil, but they can be successful in early writing and reading on a computer that speaks.

Primary Editor Plus has a speech capability, which permits language processing to occur on a computer. Students can type letters of the alphabet and see them on the screen, hear them, and then receive a printed copy of them. This visual, auditory, and tactile response is a very effective teaching support tool for anyone in early literacy stages, regardless of age.

Many early literacy processes are fostered through the use of the computer. Left-to-right directionality has historically been a difficulty, especially among students who end up being identified for special education because of their delayed reading and reversal writing. O. K. Moore reported children who taught themselves to read using computer-controlled talking typewriters in the 1950s had the directional pattern controlled for them by the action of the typewriter. In her book on Becoming Literate, noted reading recovery creator and literacy authority Marie Clay wonders if the computer might provide a child with control of the directional schema, and if it does, states that this may help young children to establish the motor habits and space orientation to reading and writing. She recognizes that researchers need to find the effect of computer use in this area. This project, with its large sample of children involved, proved that students indeed do acquire the left–right directionality so vital to reading as they subliminally are exposed to it in their daily writings. There was no evidence of any students that had directionality problems after writing with the computer all year. Reversals were also things of the past as students' daily exposure to print helped them a great deal with correct letter formation when they were writing with implements other than the computer.

Good readers seem to learn a pattern of movements for the visual scanning of print. Reading and listening to text on the computer screen was shown to help learners achieve this pattern of movements. Children previously labeled dyslexic and ADD were among those showing the most improvement in writing and growth in self-esteem due to their new vision of themselves as successful writers rather than classroom failures. Marie Clay writes about observational records of the first year of reading behaviors, showing that all children passed through a stage of locating words one by one, as if the identification of written with oral symbols were better emphasized by finger-pointing (Clay 1991). The value of kinesthetic exploration to supplement visual information at an early stage of reading instruction has been recognized by authorities such as Grace Fernald (Fernald 1943). The computer provides this kinesthetic and tactile experience, the highlighting of words as they are read on the screen supports the finger-pointing needed for early learners. One-to-one correspondence was quickly fostered in all students as they read back the stories they wrote daily.

Other discoveries made about children's writings with the assistance of the computer were that the topics they wrote about when they were free to process their own language on the keyboard were much more varied, interesting, and many times more personal than the stories the students in the control classroom would dictate for their teachers to write down for them. This phenomena of disclosing more personal information on a computer confirms reports from psychologists working with the Eliza software program, a counseling program that uses artificial intelligence (AI) to respond to questions asked of the patient. The psychologists discovered that patients will disclose much more personal and relevant information to a computer than to a live counselor. The computer is nonjudgmental and therefore more risk-free. The body language of a counselor or teacher, or their words or raised eyebrows, might convey a message that you are not safe to write or say what you really feel. This was a benefit for students who had seemed withdrawn in the classroom and rarely spoke in class discussion. Teachers found that the children shared much more about their ideas, thoughts, and feelings in print when writing on the computer daily. The teachers unanimously felt they knew their students better when reading their daily computer writings than they had ever known past groups of students.

Since writing is done individually most of the time (sometimes pairs or groups would choose to collaborate on a story together), and there are no wrong answers, students can all write at their present developmental level. This means that, regardless of level, they all produce a print-out and draw a picture and feel equally successful as authors. This boast to their self-esteem is a very important change from the years where we did three reading groups and named the groups Redbirds, Bluebirds, and Buzzards. Students who were Buzzards were well aware of their low status of learning in the classroom, and their self-esteem suffered accordingly.

Students can type their names, words in the environment, and those words in their listening, speaking vocabulary on the first day of school; print them; illustrate them; and take them home as evidence of their new-found membership in the literacy club. When I was a new first-grade teacher 25 years ago, and a student asked me on the first day of school when he would learn to read, I had to say, "Not until we teach you these 325 readings skills on our scope and sequence reading chart." Dejectedly the student walked back to his desk and his worksheet on the letter a. Today, on the first day of kindergarten or first grade, when a child asks a teacher when will they learn to read, the teacher can say, "Today." They enter the door a kindergarten or first-grade student and leave the Writing to Read lab as an author! The self-esteem enhancement and efficacy of producing adult-style, professional print at age 3–7 is empowering and inspires students to want to write daily, just as the smile and excitement of a parent during early language development fosters continued language progress. This element of empowerment for early literacy learners is one of the great strengths of a program of this kind.

In the Information Age, equity issues and equal access of technology is important for all learners, however those needing eye–hand coordination support, ESL students, those who were recommended for special education or Chapter 1 programs, and the gifted, who are often bored with standard approaches, really benefit most from the integration of technology in the classroom. The use of technology allows all learners to produce the same quality professional print and feel success in written communication at the vital early stages.

The English language is not a phonemically regular one because it is an amalgam of so many different languages. There are over 100,000 different spelling patterns to master when learning this language. Therefore it is quite normal when children are creating their own stories that they will often use invented spelling or spelling that sounds like the word they mean but does not follow conventional spelling rules. Just like the baby who starts with approximations of words and receives enthusiasm and support, these early attempts at writing, when they convey the child's meaningful message, should also be enthusiastically accepted. Often called inventive spelling, this is a stage in the process of developing written literacy, just as those early approximations of speech was. Similarly, as an adult should not resort to baby talk when modeling appropriate speech for a child, the adults never teach inventive spelling, they always model standard English (book) spelling. It is just a matter of acceptance of the meaningful message, whether written or spoken, at this stage of development. The teacher always models book spelling in her writing and children read trade books daily and are exposed to the book spelling there. Many teachers encouraged children to keep a file of the words they want to learn with book spelling. Sylvia Ashton Warner in her book, *Teacher*, describes how she successfully taught Maori children to read using key vocabulary cards of words they wanted to learn. This technique would work very well in this environment (Warner 1986).

Although teachers were happy to have phonemic software available, they also insisted, as the professional educator in charge of the class, to reserve the right to use this software and adapt it to the needs of their particular students as they felt appropriate. Generally speaking approximately two-thirds of the children in a classroom already have internalized the phoneme sounds of our language and the alphabetic principle before they enter the classroom. It is about one-third or less of the group that needs additional assistance in this area. This software provides it. The teachers correlated the use of the phonics sounds with the literature being read by students and the stories being written. Some teachers developed ways to integrate the cycle words presented in the program into thematic teaching and subsequently the writing process of the students. If used according to student interest and need to know, the graphics can be interesting and the subliminal learning of left-to-right directionality, alphabet knowledge, exposure to sight words, and knowledge that letters come together and produce words of recognizable objects in the environment are all useful learning. The graphics visually illustrating the cycle words and the auditory reinforcement of the spoken word are motivating for many students. The computer presentation of the graphic illustration of the word as well as the symbol and sound of it aid concept formation and retention.

As the software improves and becomes interactive, students will be able choose their own words to view and select the graphics they want to represent them. This will provide an even better language learning environment. There is a definite need for the software presenting the phoneme sounds in this program to be updated and presented in a more meaningful fashion. The Discus software that presents talking books in several languages and is interactive is a step towards this type of powerful new learning tool.

The networking of computers in the classroom was found by the teachers to be extremely effective. Networks allow teachers access to many software programs without having to load and unload disks. Teachers can design classes that use specific software packages that meet the needs of the learners in their group. Networks greatly decrease the workload in the classroom.

Telecommunications software and access to a network, such as America Online, allows teachers to be able to communicate from classroom to classroom, district to district, and with other students globally.

The level of knowledge of technology use among the teachers and their integration of technology into their curriculum and classroom day was probably one of the most positive results of this study.

> *Even though this is my first child in school, I know she is ahead in reading and writing ability due to this outstanding program! In kindergarten she came home and read to me, I had no idea she could read, and it's just progressed from there—the sky's the limit and she's able to express in writing whatever she feels! We feel very privileged to have had the opportunity to be in the WTR program!*
>
> *(Kindergarten parent, Nightingale School)*

School Districts Involved in the Simi Star Project
Simi Valley Unified, Justin Elementary, Crestview Elementary
Orcutt Unified, Nightingale School
Hueneme School District, Williams School, Haycock School
Ventura School District, Loma Vista School, Portola School
Oxnard School District, Juanita School, Harrington School
Santa Barbara School District, Franklin School

It is recommended that more schools adopt a qualitative approach to program evaluation in addition to the quantitative test data they already collect. This study made it quite evident that the writing process growth, the increased self-esteem essential to the learning process, and reading attitude are all factors not measured in traditional standardized reading tests. Ironically, most of the research studies cited by Slavin's mega-analysis were of this type (Slavin 1990).

Teachers contributed case studies pertaining to students they felt really had made dramatic progress in literacy using this system. The following ones are examples of what each teacher saw happen again and again.

Dorian's Story
Dorian was a kindergarten child, multicultural learner, child of divorce, and visibly unhappy. The teacher introduced him to the word processing function of Primary Editor Plus. He immediately learned how to log on to the network and could be found working diligently each day writing stories on the computer. The program allowed each child to write 15 filename stories. One morning I observed him at the computer, he wrote a story and then named it Leo8, the computer responded that there already was a Leo8 and Dorian quickly changed the filename to Leo9. I said to him, "Good work, Leo," at which time Dorian looked up at me in disgust and said, "My name isn't Leo, it's Dorian!" "Then why did you name it Leo?" I asked. "Because I already wrote 15 stories under Dorian," he replied, "So now I call myself Leo!" (Pretty good problem solving for a five year old!)

The teacher was still concerned about Dorian's unhappiness in the class due to his parents' divorce. She brought in a literature story, "My Mother's House, My Father's House," that tells about children of divorce and how both parents still love the child, and the divorce is not the child's fault. After listening intently to the teacher's story, Dorian went to the computer. I AM MYSELF he typed out and then drew a happy picture of himself. He brought it to the teacher and read it to her. "Now I understand," he said. "They both love me and I am myself." The teacher noticed a breakthrough in Dorian's personality due to his ability to write out his thoughts and feelings on the word processor. This empowering and validating feature of the writing children do on the computer when it is available to them in the classroom is a strength of this program.

Matthew's Story

Matthew was a first grader in a K/1/2 combination class. He was in this same teacher's class as a kindergartner as well. Matthew completed all 10 cycles of Writing to Read last year. This year he repeated only the last 5 cycles. Matthew entered school last year unsure and lacking confidence. He was very capable academically, but he had not "unlocked" the key to written communication. He felt that just by attending school he was going to make the transition from a nonreader/writer to a reader and writer. When he didn't magically begin reading upon entering the door, he became very cautious and unsure of himself. At the beginning of the year, Matthew would not make any attempts if he was not absolutely sure he could complete a task. If asked to read or write something, he would say he couldn't write or he couldn't read. With the help of Writing to Read and the risk-free atmosphere, his self-confidence and attitude began to change. Writing to Read gave Matthew the key he needed to unlock the literacy door. It also allowed him not to know everything. He learned that it was O.K. to know only a few sounds or to read only a few words. He no longer felt that he was incapable of these tasks, rather he was taking the "baby" steps necessary to really understand reading and writing. Once Matthew started writing, we couldn't stop him. He knew that all his attempts would be accepted and praised, and he was able to see his own learning taking place. Matthew has become comfortable and capable as a writer. He knows that our language is a crazy combination of spelling patterns and "non-patterns" and that over time he will learn all the skills necessary to become a "book" speller. He enjoys writing and reading his writing, and he enjoys the compliments and attention he receives from his efforts. He is a true author!

Miguel's Story

Miguel was nine years old and from Mexico. He had never attended school. As a non-English speaker he was sent to a first-grade classroom to work in the WTR program for a portion of the morning; he spent the rest of the day with his age mates in a fourth-grade classroom. After several months using the computer and the English cycle words in the WTR classroom, he learned English rapidly and the computer easily and well. He began to tutor first-grade students. After six months he returned to the fourth-grade classroom, where he is not only a successful student but the computer aide for that classroom. His self-esteem blossomed, and we were told by his principal that when Miguel entered his school, everyone looked at him as a high-risk student, and he is now one of the fourth-grade computer mentors! The principal was pleased and amazed at this success. The empowerment of the computer gives a boost to self-esteem and the individualized approach to ESL allows learners to work in a risk-free environment at their own rate.

The most convincing conclusion, however, came from the voices of the kindergarten and first-grade students and therefore is not considered an effective evaluation tool for judging the efficacy of this program. (That's ironic, too, isn't it!) But I believe the reason we are educators is for the successful learning of our students, who are our clients, after all. So I will share with you what some of the students had to say about this writing opportunity that they experienced.

Sean, a first grader, highly intelligent but with limited motor skill, said, "It's much easier for me to write stories on the computer. I love it, I can finally write stories about myself." Caroline, a first grader says, "I like the computer, it's like a friend that helps you write your stories." Kaela, another first grader, loves Stories and More software and says, "It makes you like stories more and become a better reader."

Damien, a kindergarten student, who made the biggest impression on me, said it best after he finished reading the paper he wrote on the computer about himself. "I can read," he said with a big grin, "Yes, I can read, look at this story I printed out!"

Kindergarten and first-grade children in the Simi Star Writing to Read in the Classroom Project during the 1991–1992 school year made greater gains in literacy skills (writing and reading) and reported a more positive reading attitude than comparable kindergarten and first grade children who received traditional instruction. The outcome measures used in the evaluation project reflect that this new adaptation of Writing to Read specifically for the classroom setting enhanced the development of essential literacy skills for kindergarten and first graders, regardless of socioeconomic status, cultural group, gender or handicapping condition.

Follow-Up Study of the Simi Star Project

The principals of each of the schools involved in the 1991 experimental Writing to Read projects were contacted four years later to learn about their experiences with the program, including whether the implementation had been successful and whether technology growth continued in their schools. Pat Eggleton, from Nightingale School in Orcutt Unified School District, Santa Maria, California, reported that Writing to Read was now integrated in all the kindergarten and first-grade classrooms of her school. All the second-grade classrooms had computers and the follow-up program, Writing to Write. She stated that the original K–1 pilot project, with its focus and emphasis on technology, had been very successful. Teachers at other grades were enthusiastic about having technology in their classrooms. Parents who witnessed the successful learning of their 5 and 6 year olds demanded technology in their children's classrooms as the children advanced in the grades. As a result, implementation of technology in the classrooms occurred schoolwide. Eggleton found that technology addressed all children's needs. The vision of Orcutt School District Superintendent Jack Garvin helped support principals like Eggleton and made his school district a Challenge District. (A Challenge District is one chosen by California State Superintendent Delaine Eastin as one that is on the cutting edge of educational reform.)

Over in Oxnard, an enterprising and avid computer-using principal named Tony Zubia now has computers in all his school's classrooms and is adding CDs, lasers, and Internet access. His school's participation in the Simi Star Project was the catalyst for the whole-school technology integration. The school has its own home page on the Internet (www.oxnard.sd.org).

Mary Samples, who was principal of Williams School in Hueneme School District, has been promoted to the district level. However, she confirmed that her schools' participation in the Simi Star Project was a key factor in how technology has now blossomed in many of the schools.

Summary

The examination of learning activities in the classroom needs to be legitimatized as a research methodology. The dynamic nature of social interactions in the classroom setting provides more important data and insights about the influence on literacy development of the social community, the materials being used, and the kinds of interaction patterns than one-on-one interviews provide (Goodman 1990).

The Simi Star Project was a good example of how our exploration about literacy must be based on research that comes directly from the classroom setting and within the real, dynamic context in which learning occurs. Further research must focus on the learner and what sort of classroom environment, teacher facilitation, and peer interaction is the best for each child's literacy development.

The search for knowledge about what children know about literacy development must continue. Many languages and many sociocultural climates must be examined in order to support the universality of the ways in which children come to know literacy (Goodman 1990). Through the use of the language machine in classrooms around the world, researchers have made a start toward discovering the universal empowerment children experience in early reading and writing. The search must continue. Children have much to tell us and many stories to write.

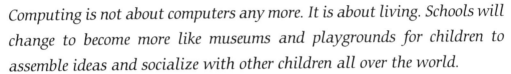

Chapter 10

The Problem of Change in the Culture of School

Computing is not about computers any more. It is about living. Schools will change to become more like museums and playgrounds for children to assemble ideas and socialize with other children all over the world.

Negroponte 1995

This chapter discusses why the culture of school is resistant to change and why computer technology has been accepted in this culture only so far as it supports existing practice. This explains the early acceptance of the computer into the schools as a drill machine or game machine only. Computers were used to support the medieval concept of information as something that is stored in a fixed form in a repository designed exclusively for that purpose. The fundamental instinct of durable organizations is to resist change: That is why they are durable. However, as the values of society change, schools must change. If they do not, they will be replaced. Despite the headlines announcing discontent with our educational system and an apparent widespread desire for something different, the educational establishment, including most of the research community, remains largely committed to the educational philosophy of the late nineteenth and early twentieth centuries. So far, none of those who challenge these hallowed traditions has been able to loosen the hold of the educational establishment on how children are taught (Papert 1993).

In 1984, after an extensive looks at schools, John Goodlad wrote,

> a condition to which our system of schooling has responded sluggishly, is the stunningly swift advance of technology in virtually all aspects of life. The end is not in sight. Persons who just a few years ago were operating elevators, attending to parking lots, and selling newspapers on the street corners have been replaced by buttons to push and boxes which respond to the insertion of plastic cards. The schools, compared with other institutions, have responded very little to this technological revolution. But it is difficult to believe that schools can have a future apart from technology (Goodlad 1984).

This message, delivered more than 12 years ago, has not changed a great deal. The amount of technology in schools is far short of its established use—not someday, but already in our society. The current trend of homeschooling and other options is growing. The schooling of the future cannot be an adaptation of the old industrial model, it must be a new vision. Goodlad states that our old notion of the home and church and school as our educating agencies and institutions must be expanded to include the new media of communication and distance learning, technology, and television. Educators have an important task in determining how this new vision will be developed and implemented.

As technology advances rapidly, what directions should it take? Each day, better software is developed to be used in the classroom by educators. The newest version of KidWorks Deluxe is a multimedia creativity kit that combines word processor and paint program into one program. Combined with KidPhonics, a publishing center like the Writing to Read Innovation can be designed in any classroom using any hardware. Educators must be wise consumers, demanding the materials they know work, rather than saying to vendors, "We don't know what to get."

How Innovations Change to Fit the Existing Culture of the School

For many years, basal reader series have dominated the reading programs of U.S. schools. Millions of dollars are spent every time a school district purchases these standardized, controlled texts for all students. Book company executives wine and dine school superintendents and members of textbook selection committees. When we gather research about how children learn to read by selecting materials and reading the good literature books, textbook publishers respond with selections, adaptations, or excerpts from literature books—sort of a condensed book approach to good literature! (One of the worst examples of publishers misusing original literature is the publisher who reprinted Judy Blume's *The One in the Middle Is a Green Kangaroo*. The publisher changed Freddie, the boy in the story, to Maggie, a girl, to balance gender representation. They took Blume's descriptive language, "Freddie felt like the peanut butter in the middle of a peanut butter and jelly sandwich," and substituted, "Maggie was the one in the middle" to simplify the language. However, salespeople proudly told committees that Judy Blume's literature book was contained in the series!

Why would anyone want an adaptation when it's easy to purchase real books for the classroom? In fact some school districts have begun buying class sets of good literature books to use in the classrooms. But once again, old ways take over innovation. As if teachers would be unable to handle children reading self-selected materials, an approach advocated long ago by Dr. Jeannette Veatch (Veatch 1959), districts have called together committees who have decided which literature books will be used by each grade level. Suddenly, hard-and-fast rules evolve around these selections. If the book is selected for sixth grade, a child better not read it in any other grade! Once again, the student's interest and need to know falls before adult choices and simplified procedures.

In one fifth-grade classroom, the teacher proudly said the entire class was reading *The Summer of the Swans*. Students were supposed to be silently reading a chapter of the book, but one boy looked as bored as any child in a basal reader program. Asked what was wrong, he said, "I wish I could read the *Phantom Toll Booth*, but the teacher says that is a sixth-grade selection and I can't read it till next year. I hate this!" After the reading, all students had to respond to the same questions, just as they have for many years with basal selections. This is just one example of how an innovation can be poorly used.

How to Make Implementation Work in Your School

In an investigation into why one school's Writing to Read program was successful while another school's (in the same district) was not, certain critical factors were identified (Pezoldt 1989). The factors that contribute to successful implementation are:

1. The principal's involvement. This was a major factor in the success of the program. The principal's rapport with staff and involvement in training sessions facilitated the smooth transition.

2. Teachers worked as a team and were flexible and willing to change.

3. There were sufficient funds to hire aides and commit to training.

The authors concluded that as more and more schools implement innovations like Writing to Read and other technology programs into the curriculum, it is important they address key issues prior to the actual adoption and implementation.

The first key issue is the amount of involvement the principal will have with the program. This includes attending all training sessions with the staff, being involved in staff meetings dealing with the new program, and having times to deal with concerns from the community as well as the staff. There needs to be a general feeling of support and enthusiasm from the principal. The second key issue is the staff and how open it is to change. How the training of teachers will take place must be determined. Finally, adequate funds and personnel to provide sufficient assistance to the teachers before, during and after implementation must be provided. Literature on implementation theory indicates that these areas consistently stand out as important areas of consideration.

Despite revolutionary advances in the field of educational computing, technology is simply a tool. Potentially powerful and stimulating, the computer is only an inert object that can never substitute for the personal touch of the classroom teacher. How teachers implement computer use is critical. Without proper integration of computers into the curriculum, the benefits of technology to empower students and enhance their learning can not be fully accomplished.

Sister Agnes Vieno, coordinator for Los Angeles Archdiocese Schools, offered several suggestions she used in carrying out a successful, seven-year implementation covering 120 schools and many more classrooms. She found that the most important component for a successful school and classroom implementation of technology is educator's support. She required educators of a school considering technology implementation, from administrator to all concerned teachers, to visit at least two school sites that have successfully implemented the program. Then they must write a proposal describing their school populations, the educational value they feel the program offers, the configuration of computers they will choose for their classrooms, and how their plan will help the literacy of their students. They should write a follow-up report in one year, if their proposal is approved. She finds that this process creates ownership of the program, which is essential to success.

A district coordinator needs to be identified. Coaching for implementation, frequent teacher training, and online teacher discussion groups are also parts of a success program. Giving teachers software and access to computers to use in their own learning is also very important. Teachers must model using computers in their own writing and information gathering, just as teachers and parents need to model writing and reading behaviors.

The last, and perhaps most important, condition for successful implementation is the attitude of the educators concerned. All need to be lifelong learners, eager to learn new innovations and ideas, excited to share them with students but also willing to learn from students.

Educators still have the responsibility to create the best possible learning environment in which children of the twenty-first century can learn.

Major Changes Needed in Attitudes About Learners

All children, regardless of culture or socioeconomic level, have stories to tell. They might not be the stories commonly heard: They might be stories of escaping from Vietnam with their cousins. They might be stories of moving into a condemned building and saving cans and bottles to cash in to get money to eat. Regardless of content, all children have thoughts in their minds and stories in their hearts. In *Growing Up Literate: Learning from Inner-City Families*, Denny Taylor describes just such youngsters (Taylor and Dorsey-Gaines 1988). Educators must view all children as desiring to learn, and with stories to tell. Then—lo and behold!—we will find it is true. Listen to voices of the children who surround you. They will tell you their life stories.

Funding for Technology

The near-total lack of funding for technological development and innovation in the education sector can best (and probably only) be remedied by reallocating a substantial portion of existing education budgets. Because state governments provide about half of K–12 funding in the United States, and a larger share of total higher education funding, states are in the best position to swiftly and effectively close education's technology gap (Perelman 1992). Parents and educators alike need to contact state legislators to be sure they are aware of the importance and need for this funding. Schools cannot afford to lag behind the technology already established in the culture they are preparing students to join. Without funding, none of the technology needed in the classrooms will be purchased.

But, contrary to what many administers bemoan, it is not inherently impossible for public schools to use their own money to purchase technology. Philip Grignon, superintendent of the South Bay Union Schools, an elementary district in Imperial Beach, California, demonstrated how it can be done. Under his leadership, this district has invested more than $3 million of school budget funds in classroom computer networks. Grignon's determination to help the students he serves has made this happen for his school district. Innovators like Grignon and Dr. Jack Garvin of Orcutt Unified School District, Santa Maria, California, who is putting computers in every classroom at every school in his district, need not be a rarity. Our schools need administrators with their vision.

Changes in Schools' Writing and Reading Environment

The researchers reporting in this book have a total of over 120 years experience working with beginning readers. We have survived every major theory, method, and approach to reading popular from the 1950s until 1996. We have tried many of them and observed many others. Many were honest attempts by researchers to find the one ingredient that could make a difference for all children. Some have tried to teach children to crawl again, some gave them letters in color, some had them learn letters from inflatable characters, some required them to parrot sounds like mynah birds. One particular off-the-wall method had students wearing blindfolds to occlude a modality. Many of these methods were devised strictly for marketing benefit without testing or research. They were purchased because it was the popular thing to do or it was a hit at a reading convention or was being sold by an Elmer Gantry of education.

Perhaps because these methods focused on only one part of the literacy process, they missed the most important lesson about how children learn. Literacy is a total process that embraces listening, speaking, writing, reading, visual knowledge and social interaction. It is a complicated, integrated process. No small part of this process, no matter how attractively packaged, can make the process happen. There are great universals of human development, but each child takes on the task of developing his or her own oral, written, and spoken literacy through a unique genetic and experiential combination that no others share. In order to support each of these developing literacy learners, knowledgeable teachers must use a combination of strategies. Parents, who know that each child is unique, can provide different types of encouragement and support to each of their own children.

Is the Talking Computer the Best Reading Method?

The single best reading method for children may never exist. Given the enormous range of students—their interests, experiences, and circumstances—it would be foolhardy to believe that there is a magic method or protocol or group of phoneme sounds that will turn all students into writers and readers. The talking computer is not a reading method, it is a tool to write with, a tool to solve problems with. Students using it design their own method to learn and write about their world.

Tens of thousands of research studies have failed to isolate a single, best method of teaching reading. No study has demonstrated that an ideal method exists (Smith 1983). What students need to learn to speak, write, and read are competent role models of speaking, writing, and reading who help them make sense of and use language. When these competent role models also use word processors to communicate and make sense of their environment and help students see how these tools can make it easier for them to tell their story, to make sense of print, to communicate with others, learning happens. However, even the most wonderful device is subject to misuse in the hands of poor teachers and role models. Frank Smith says, "Some teachers could make students anxious handing out free milk. Teachers who need to be told the best method would probably not be capable of succeeding with it, even if it existed" (Smith 1983).

A good teacher uses all the tools available to construct an environment that is conducive to learning. No one needs to write a script for this teacher's thoughts, words, or writing. This teacher is a reader, a writer, a problem solver, a cheerleader for learning. This teacher can be trusted to take charge and be responsible for supporting the literacy learning of each student.

No one kit, workbook, approach, method, or procedure is the magic cure for all children. In fact, there are as many different ways human beings learn to write and read as there are human beings learning the task. The United States Office of Education Comparative First Grade Studies (the most extensive comparisons of beginning reading approaches ever conducted) found no method superior to any other. Superior results, if any, were attributed to the teacher (Chall 1983).

Good teachers constantly search for good methods to use with each child they are charged with helping grow to literacy. As the year 2000 approaches, educators should turn away from gimmicks and turn to children. Observational data from Piaget, Froebel, Montessori, Holdaway, Calkins, Graves, Taylor and Gaines, Smith, Krashen, Veatch, and Van Allen provide insight into how children really learn to write and read. Rather than continuing the fruitless fight between the For and Against Phonics Pholks, teachers must concentrate on creating an environment of learning in which each individual child can grow at his or her own rate. Such teachers need support and the power and tools to make individual decisions about how to facilitate the writing and reading growth of each child.

Classrooms of the Future

Schools need to include classrooms equipped, with educators who understand how human beings learn most effectively, that is, in a supportive environment and with a curriculum that centers on students' interests and need to know. Such an educator loves and accepts all students, regardless of culture or learning strengths and weaknesses. Schools need educators who recognize the talking computer and technology as an important learning tool, a tool that brings visuals to the fingertips of students and helps create a classroom that is truly a collaborative learning environment. As you read this book, share this message, and prepare such learning environments in your schools and homes, you will provide children like Codey, David, Nicholas, Orlando—and all children who have struggled or are struggling to make sense of print—a better start at literacy. They will become an author on their first day of school. Like Damien, who at age five typed out his first message "I am ME," children will proudly claim their place as a member of the literacy club. The language machine is a tool that helps children express the many ideas in their minds and hearts. Help every one of your students find their written voice through this powerful tool.

Chapter 11

Future Directions

I am not an advocate for frequent changes in laws and constitutions, but laws and institutions go hand in hand with the progress of the human mind. As that becomes more developed, more enlightened, as new discoveries are made, new truths discovered and manners and opinions change, with the change of circumstances, institutions must advance also to keep pace with the times. We might as well require a man to wear still the coat which fitted him when a boy as civilized society to remain ever under the regimen of their barbarous ancestors.

Thomas Jefferson

As I am completing this book, I am visiting schools and phoning teachers to see how much implementation of talking word processors has taken place since my early research 10 years ago. When I checked my e-mail, the following message made my day:

> Dear Jean,
>
> I am using technology in my classroom and schoolwide. We are at a newer school (3 yrs old) in Centralia School District. I am the early literacy mentor. I have used KidWorks 2 both at school and with my 6 year old at home. Great program. It was the first that my son was able to do. He has been working with it since age 4. Our school has 54 Macs, many with CD-ROMs. We just purchased WiggleWorks in both Spanish and English and I am anxious to use it with our 2 and 3rd grade Title one kids. We run an afterschool program using a lot of Reading Recovery strategies along with writing editing and then word-processing their own stories. We have set up grade level goals for our kids. Our goal is to produce computer literate students by the end of 6th grade. It is quite exciting. Would love to hear more about your book. Our

school has received 2 grants for technology which has helped us greatly. We are linked through e-mail so no more long memos in our boxes and it has shortened our staff meetings. A lot of us are online from home as well.

I think the greatest gain has been that we are so much closer as a staff now. Personal messages to colleagues pulls everyone together. Would love to tap into your insights and knowledge about computer use with kids.

Happy New Year, Donna aka Teachkgn

Teachers like Donna will make it happen both at home and at school. It has been a long wait, but it has been worth it. Codey's was a lone voice in 1983, but he is joined by thousands of other excited voices as they print their first ideas on the computer, hear it read back to them and exclaim, "I can read! Look at what I wrote, I'm an author!"

Future Possibilities

A *Los Angeles Times* front-page story entitled, "Help for Kids with Learning Disabilities" (January 5, 1996) described what a bicoastal research team from Rutgers University and the University of San Francisco feel is a breakthrough therapy for learning disabled youngsters. They describe these children as children who have trouble understanding the spoken word and go on to develop reading problems characteristic of dyslexia. In their study, they used specially designed computer games, CD-ROM books, and audiotapes. Using computers to present programs that accentuate and lengthen the sounds and then gradually reduce them to normal, the researchers have been able to help the children reach near-normal language capabilities in a few weeks. The sample is very small, including only children who were severely delayed in language and reading skills. The team is now organizing a much larger trial of thousands of children. This is an exciting example of the brightest of minds working to solve problems. But even more powerful is their inclusion of a web site. After reading the article, I connected to the research team's Web site (http://www.ld.ucsf.edu). From this site I can join their mailing list, ask questions, send ideas, and become a resource. This could never have happened 14 years ago.

Amazing things can happen now with the collaboration and advanced learning of all professionals solving problems together. Whether it is the teacher or the students in the classroom, the Internet will bring us all closer to solutions and unite the brainpower of millions to work toward improved education for all.

"Being literate means to be able to talk with and listen with others to interpret texts, say what they mean, link them to personal experience and with other texts, argue with them and make predictions from them, develop future scenarios, compare and evaluate related situations, and know that the practice of all these literate abilities is practical" (Heath 1983). With that definition in mind, educators and parents need to study literacy with computers as an important feature of the setting, a feature that changes literate practices but adds to them, not replacing, but enhancing writing, reading, and communicating. We must be avid observers of children, for they have much to teach us about how they interact with technology and what advances will support their learning. Children should always be our curriculum informants and our guides to what they need to learn most effectively.

Issues of equity or access to technology for all children are paramount. Clearly the issues of culture, education, and technology merge at the crossroads of the twenty-first century. Do we plan for the common good by enabling all students to navigate difference, develop intellectually and academically, and gain expertise in employing technology for enhancing democratic participation (Cummins and Sayers 1995)? The hope for the next generation is that we do.

In describing his vision for a basic school, Ernest Boyer states that, despite its great potential, technology in most elementary school classrooms in the United States is shockingly deficient. It is shocking that almost every other enterprise in this country—from banks to airlines to hotels to places of commerce—has, quite literally, been transformed by technology. But if all the technology were suddenly removed from schools, hardly anyone would notice. How serious can we be about educating our children for the next century when we've barely equipped them for this one, he asks (Boyer 1995)? We need educators with vision to make the changes in schools now. We need computers in every classroom, one computer for every five children, at least. We need VCRs, telecommunication, printers, phone lines and a teacher's presentation workstation. Then we will have the literacy environment children need to learn and a workplace in which the very best of teachers can guide them on their way. In the end, it is the educators who will make the difference for every child who walks through a classroom door.

Research on the brain shows a language-learning window from birth to 10 years. Circuits in the auditory cortex, representing the sounds that form words, are wired by the age of one. The more words a child hears by two, the larger the vocabulary will grow. The musical brain develops from ages three to ten (Begley 1996). Music trains the brain for higher forms of thinking. New computer programs like the Living Books, which combine music and interactive language arts, plus the talking word processor for learning languages starting at age three, will bring increased literacy to all children.

Education of the Future

How will technology impact children's education in the year 2021? Perhaps one of its most positive effects is teaching children to think more effectively. We have had a tendency to categorize children into smart and dumb people when, in fact, it is often a question of context and experience (Parham 1988). The high motivational state induced in children working with good educational software, coupled with the emergence of a global network of databases that allow the child access to information with unprecedented ease, must have an impact on the understanding children develop of the world they live in and, for that matter, in understanding themselves. Children encouraged to write their own programs will develop intellectual skills of precision and logic, a systematic and orderly method for producing work, and a much more sophisticated approach to the methods of solving problems. Computers will enhance the creative impulses of children (Steuben 1995). It is expected that the new technologies will transform, not merely supplement, students' learning.

If anything can be predicted about computers and literacy, it is that some people will oversell the technology as a positive force and that others will decry it as an abomination. Perhaps the most we can hope for is a continued reliance on talented teachers acquiring an informed exuberance (Chandler and Marcus 1985) and the young children excelling on computers in the home growing up and showing us the way. Together they will be major forces in making the most of whatever the technology has to offer us in this new information age.

Applying technology to existing schools, like just one more of many band-aids, is not the solution. How then do we restructure to meet the needs of education in the Information Age? Goodlad suggests one alternative is to consider the other institutions and agencies of education, like radio, television, and the computer. He calls for melding the schools with different institutions and agencies. Community education becomes not just schools opening up their facilities and extending their resources, but an ecosystem of institutions and agencies conscious of their responsibility for developing the knowledge, values, skills, and habits of a free people (Goodlad 1984).

Other educators suggest that the computer and ancillary technology will invade the home and alter the education system in a way unparalleled in previous education history (Stonier and Conlin 1985). "Computers are a new kind of writing machine for authors, a new kind of brush for painters, a new kind of instrument for musicians. The computer screen is a different material for artists to work on. Computers have helped artists create new worlds of animation, of simulations and games, new kinds of maps, new kinds of models, new kinds of landscapes. Computers can help everyone who wants to become more creative" (Smith 1990).

New software is constantly being created, and each generation of software builds upon preceding generations. Although first-generation software was little more than electronic workbook sheets, the newest software is lightyears better. IBM has just introduced a new writing program called, Write Along. In an introduction to this new interactive writing program, Dr. Elizabeth Sulzby notes that the software provides features, such as text-to-speech at the child's demand, instant switches of fonts, size, and color in reformatting form; flawless editing; multiple copies of originals; expanded and consistent examples of letter–sound matches at a mouse click; and point-and-click access to visuals and print. "Children easily expect all these forms in their daily lives, and we adults are learning from and along with the children" (Sulzby 1994).

As new programs are developed, they will be able to sense the learning style and ability level of the learner without the learner even being aware of it. Present-day programs for studying for the GMAT test provides the student with questions tailored to the answers of the previous questions asked. By being geared to the learner, the questions become more understandable.

Marshall McLuhan declared that the world is in the process of becoming a global village. His theory was that visual literacy fragmented humanity into specialties which collected in cities, but all would be reversed by the "tribal drum" of electronic communications, and village-style connectivity would return on a planetary scale. The science fiction writer William Gibson imagines that all who live by computers will one day commingle in a jointly created virtual reality (Brand 1987).

Perhaps the homeschooling movement will flourish, and school sites themselves will become places for socialization, debate, and community activities, while information is delivered to the home and distance learning is the mode of transmission of knowledge and coaching by experts. Then, parents would be the primary on-site person to encourage, praise, and inspire.

But having parents, teachers, and researchers who observe how children learn, listen to their voices, read their stories, and understand how early literacy comes about is not enough. Unless world leaders, national leaders, and state and local leaders who fund and make decisions about how school environments are created, no fundamental change will occur. When the education policy makers bend to special interest groups and produce fragmented reports that reflect political bias and not the reality of children's learning; when test results and textbook sales continue to drive the curriculum; when the band-aid solutions are implemented to appease constituents, then children's voices go unheard and their writings unread. Each of us has a responsibility to keep that from happening.

We are at a marvelous juncture in the freeing of the human brain's potential for learning. The three to six year olds are eager and willing to point out the way. Many new exciting discoveries about the power of learning are being discovered daily and communicated globally online. Just as we feel we have found a solution to help those learners who have not before been able to get meaning from print, we have a new sort of visual knowledge appearing on the horizon—that is, multimedia and visual presentations that children can create to reflect their knowledge. This will provide a whole new way of learning, one that sometimes is devoid of print. Whatever the future holds for the next generation, we must all have as our major concern early literacy and the language machine that can help make it attainable for all.

Appendix A

Criteria for Scoring
Writing Samples

Level Explanation

6   Ideas are very well developed and expressed. The writing has a fully developed structure, which may or may not be narrative. The ideas are connected logically and they are well organized. There is good sentence variety and expression.

5   Ideas are fairly well developed and expressed. The writing has a discernible structure. The ideas are connected logically, but they are not so fully developed or so well organized as score 6 papers.

4   Ideas are only loosely connected or not developed. The structure may be disjointed, but what is provided is clearly more than a list. The ideas are relevant but are not developed or expressed well. The sentence structure may be repetitious.

3   Ideas lack development. The writing often merely lists ideas. The phrasing and the sentence structure are repetitious.

2   Ideas have little or no relationship to a topic. An idea or a list is provided. Minimal paper.

1   Only letters or unrelated simple words. All that is presented is a copy of a prompt, or words or phrases the child sees displayed in the room.

PW   Prewriting, or mock writing

Casey Observation Scales, Simi Star Project

Name of observer _____   District _____

Class _____   Total time spent in class _____

School _____   Name of teacher _____

Organization and Management

1. Classroom organization and management
   ____ computers are located in an easily accessible manner, used continually
   ____ computers are present, moderate use
   ____ computers are hard to access, little or no use

2. Computer use and student or teacher control of use
   ____ students use computers according to interest and need
   ____ teachers assign students to computers
   ____ students can only use computers at a limited specified time

3. An aide, parent volunteer, cross age tutor or other assistance at computers is available
   ____ more than one extra adult assist in classroom at any time
   ____ teacher plus cross age tutors work with computers
   ____ teacher works alone to assist students on computers

4. Students transitions to and from computer
   ____ students move to and from computer as needed
   ____ teacher has posted schedule of times for computer use
   ____ teacher uses timer and moves groups in specific time segments

5. Student responsibility on computers
   ____ students boot up computers, select program, save and print work
   ____ teacher or aide assist students in software selection and print
   ____ teacher alone loads program, prints work, chooses program, etc.

---

6. Computers are primarily used by students with which software:
   ____ Write Along
   ____ KidWorks Deluxe
   ____ Childrens Writing and Publishing
   ____ Stories and More
   ____ other

7. Students mostly use the computers as
   ____ a tool to write and think with
   ____ a drill and mastery program for phonemic sounds
   ____ a publications tool to write class newspapers and other meaningful
        classroom publications
   ____ a method to gain more information on a specific content area (which area)
   ____ a means to communicate, collaborate on projects with global peers (Internet)

8. Teachers use computers as
   ____ a tool to help facilitate student learning
   ____ a word processing tool for parent letters, school bulletins, etc.
   ____ a telecommunications tool
   ____ a record keeping or assessment tool (save student writing for portfolios)
   ____ developing lesson plan ideas and journal notes on class (kid-watching)
   ____ other

Learning Opportunities and/or Instruction

9. Student learning occurs when
   ____ students collaborate with one another on writing projects and computer use
   ____ students work independently writing on a computer and read their stories to
        one another
   ____ students take home copies of their products daily

10. Teachers observe students at computers
    ____ teacher moves around class, queries student at computer, encourages,
         scaffolds and keeps anecdotal journal notes on student progress
    ____ teacher has some limited contact with students at computers but usually
         just pertaining to troubleshooting help on computer operations
    ____ teacher works with other groups and does not have opportunity to interact
         with students at computers at all

11. Anticipatory set or motivation
    ____ students are given appropriate set and motivation to start on computers
         actively and with enthusiasm
    ____ students are given limited directions but then do work on computers
    ____ students go to computers but seem to not know what to write or do there

12. Teacher integrates curriculum areas with computers
    _____ teachers teach thematically and utilize networked computers for integration in math, science, reading, language arts, art, music, etc.
    _____ students use computers for reading/writing throughout the day
    _____ teachers use computers for reading time only an hour a day
    _____ computers are used only after other curriculum activities; as practice or activity

Evaluation

13. Portfolio assessment
    _____ teacher keeps a selection of childrens' work daily in a folder and evaluates it
    _____ teacher keeps a weekly sample of printed work in a folder and evaluates products weekly
    _____ teachers do not keep hard copies of printed work in folders
    _____ teachers keep records of all student work on CD-ROM disk

14. Parent evaluation
    _____ parents get daily copies of student's writings on the computer
    _____ parents get a weekly copy of student writing on the computer
    _____ parents do not get copies of student writing done on the computer

15. Administrator evaluation
    _____ administrator does observation of program weekly, reminds teachers to use journals, writes lesson samples and coordinates with team leader
    _____ administrator observes program occasionally and communicates with team leader
    _____ administrator seldom observes program or interacts with teachers and team leader

16. Team leader evaluation
    _____ team leaders check e-mail daily and keep contact with all teachers and administrator, gets data to project director
    _____ team leader runs their own classroom and responds to questions from other teachers
    _____ team leader just manages their own classroom with little contact with other teachers

17. Parent involvement
    _____ parents were informed by mail of meeting at school

From *Early Literacy: The Empowerment of Technology.* © 1997.
Libraries Unlimited, Inc. 1-800-237-6124.

18. Staff innovation

_____ staff (administrator, team leaders, teachers, aides, clerical) show great commitment to project and developing product materials to make Writing to Read in the Classroom support the California State Framework English Language Arts guidelines and develop professional materials that will help other sites replicate this program.

_____ classroom teacher alone has the responsibility for coming up with lesson plan ideas and keeping journal notes on this project

_____ no one at site has taken initiative to observe, write and collect product materials necessary for study.

Observer's anecdotal comments:

Writing to Read
Questionnaires

Teacher Questionnaire

Name _____ School _____

1. How many students are in your class? K____ 1____ 2____ Other____

2. How many years teaching experience have you had, including this year? ____

3. What reading program(s) do you use with Writing to Read?

   _____

   _____

   _____

4. How long have you been using WTR? _____

5. How do you feel about Writing to Read?

   Great   Poor

      1   2   3   4   5

6. How would you rate its overall effectiveness?

   Great   Poor

      1   2   3   4   5

7. How do you think the progress in reading of most of your students compares to the progress in reading of your students in previous years?

_____

_____

_____

_____

8. How do you think the progress in writing of most of your students compares to the progress in writing of your students in previous years?

_____

_____

_____

_____

9. How does the amount of time you spend on reading compare with the amount you spent in previous years?

_____

_____

_____

_____

10. How does the amount of time you spend on writing compare with the amount you spent in previous years? (Original writing rather than handwriting)

_____

_____

_____

_____

11. How would you rate the effectiveness of Writing to Read for the following groups of children?

	Great			Poor	
Above Average	1	2	3	4	5
Average	1	2	3	4	5
Below Average	1	2	3	4	5

12. What kind of feedback have you had from parents about WTR?

_____

_____

_____

_____

How much time does a typical child in your class spend in each of the following activities?

13. Reading aloud _____

14. Reading silently _____

15. Creative writing _____

16. Developing a sight vocabulary _____

17. Learning word meanings _____

18. Phonic and/or structural analysis _____

19. Penmanship _____

We are interested in your thoughts about the writing and reading skills of the children and the use of computers in education. Please check whether you agree or disagree with the following statement.

	Y	N
20. It is important today that children learn about computers and how to use them.	○	○
21. The children are progressing as well as expected.	○	○
22. Money being spent on computers should be spent on other things.	○	○
23. Too much time is spent on Writing to Read.	○	○
24. Children this age are too young to learn by computers.	○	○
25. I hope our school will continue to use Writing to Read next year.	○	○
26. Our school should emphasize reading skills more than they do at present.	○	○
27. Our school should emphasize writing skills more than they do at present.	○	○

Principal Questionnaire

1. How successfully do you feel computers (WTR) have been integrated in your K classrooms? 1st grade classrooms?

   _____

   _____

   _____

   _____

2. What are the most positive results of this project for students in your view?

   _____

   _____

   _____

   _____

3. What are the most positive results of this project for teachers in your view?

   _____

   _____

   _____

   _____

4. Most positive results for you? For parents?

   _____

   _____

   _____

   _____

5. Problems with integration of computers in classroom?

   _____

   _____

   _____

   _____

6. What will happen regarding computers in the classroom and curriculum
    integration next year?

    _____

    _____

    _____

    _____

Parent Questionnaire

1. What grade is your child in at school? _____

2. Are you familiar with the Writing to Read (WTR) Early Literacy Learning program being used in your child's class?   ○ Yes   ○ No

3. How have you learned about the WTR program?

    _____

    _____

    _____

    _____

4. In general, how do you feel about the WTR program?

    _____

    _____

    _____

    _____

5. How do you think your child feels about the WTR program?

    _____

    _____

    _____

    _____

6. How do you think your child feels about writing stories?

    _____

    _____

    _____

    _____

7. How do you think your child feels about using the computer?

    _____

    _____

    _____

    _____

8. What evidence of your child's reading and writing skills have you seen at home?
    (Please check all that apply.)
    ○ Leaves notes around the house
    ○ Reads signs, labels, books and other materials
    ○ Wants to be read to
    ○ Wants to do his/her own reading
    ○ Wants to read to other people
    ○ Writes words and stories
    ○ Shares school work and wants to read it

9. How do you think your child's progress in reading compares to your other
    children's at this grade level?

    _____

    _____

    _____

    _____

10. How do you think your child's progress in writing compares to your other
    children's at this grade level?

    _____

    _____

    _____

    _____

Many school districts are trying to integrate the use of computers into their programs
for their students. We are interested in your thoughts about the use of computers in
education. Please check whether you agree or disagree with the following statements.

	Agree	Disagree
11. It is important today that children learn about computers and how to use them as soon as possible.	○	○
12. Money should be spent on computers and technology.	○	○
13. My child has begun to make transitions to traditional spelling patterns.	○	○
14. Writing to Read is a good use of class time.	○	○
15. Children at this age should be using computers to learn.	○	○
16. My child knew how to read when school started.	○	○
17. My child knew how to write when school started.	○	○

	Agree	Disagree
18. I hope our school will continue to use the Writing to Read program being used this year.	○	○
19. Our school puts enough emphasis on reading skills.	○	○
20. Our school puts enough emphasis on writing skills.	○	○

Please feel free to write any additional comments you may have about the Writing to Read program. Thank you for your time.

From *Early Literacy: The Empowerment of Technology.* © 1997.
Libraries Unlimited, Inc. 1-800-237-6124.

Appendix D

Software Programs for Early Literacy

KidPhonics

This program presents an interactive multimedia eenvironment that provides the auditory experience necessary for reading. Through the use of music, nursery rhymes, and classic children's songs, phonics are taught in a meaningful way. This program received a 4-star rating from *Parents* magazine.

Davidson & Associates, Inc.
P.O. Box 2961
Torrance CA 90509
1-800-545-7677

KidWorks 2 or KidWorks Deluxe

This is a talking word processor program that should be the backbone of any writing/publishing literacy environment. Children do language processing, write their own language experience stories, and hear the stories read back. This program comes in a Spanish/English version and also includes fantastic graphic capabilities for creating pictures to accompany story.

Davidson & Associates, Inc.
P.O. Box 2961
Torrance CA 90509
1-800-545-7677

Writing to Read 2000

Writing to Read is a classroom writing/reading publishing center. It is an integrated literacy learning program that helps children learn to write and read naturally and at their own pace. It includes the development of the writing process through daily language experience writings and phonics taught in a meaningful literature environment.

International Business Machine (IBM) Corporation
Educational Systems
4111 Northside Parkway
Atlanta, GA 30327

Write Along

This is a sophisticated children's talking word processor program that includes graphic capabilities and is the core of a literacy center in a classroom.

International Business Machine (IBM) Corporation
Educational Systems
4111 Northside Parkway
Atlanta, GA 30327

Living Books Series

All titles in this series are excellent for three to six year olds. Interactive stories are told in English, Spanish, and Japanese. With sound effects, original music, humor, and lots of animations, these CD-ROM programs provide a whole new learning experience for young children.

Broderbund Software, Inc.
500 Redwood Blvd.
Novato, CA 94948-6121

WiggleWorks

This is an entire school early literacy program that blends elements of Reading Recovery and other programs. This program comes with 72 easy-to-read books for the classroom. Not for home use.

Scholastic Beginning Literacy System
Scholastic, Inc.
555 Broadway
New York, NY 10012

Teacher's Checklist for Integrating Technology in the Classroom

1. Visit a classroom that has integrated technology. To find out what classroom to visit, call the school district offices in your area and ask for the computer coordinator. A visit is essential, because it allows you to see how children respond to the technology.

2. Create a newsletter for parents. Include some of the information you learned from this book, add some of the Writing to Read parent comments. Explain to PTO and parents that you need help to raise money for the technology in your room. Bake sales and other fundraisers are a start. You might find a parent who works for the phone company who can donate a phone line.

3. Visit local merchants close to the school to elicit help and donations.

4. Join the Computer Using Educators group in your area. Meet other teachers and share information. Find information about grants available to fund technology.

5. Visit your local university to find out what resources it offers to educators; find out what types of computer workshops they offer as well.

6. Join an online service like America Online or CompuServe. Find the Software Review Resources on the Web at: http://www.stan-co.K12.ca.us

   Communicate with other teachers who are setting up technology-integrated classrooms all around the world.

7. Decide what you want to accomplish in your literacy center. Find the software that will do it, and then find out what sort of computers will run that software. Be proactive. Learn about the software and hardware so you can choose the components you want. Don't let someone else make that decision for you. When you have your shopping list—and funding—in hand, order the equipment.

8. Start with four to six networked computers. Put one computer workstation on your desk. Have a printer and LCD projection monitor handy to make presentations to your students.

9. Make sure you start out with a talking word processor for literacy and LOGO writer for math concepts. That's the foundation. Add CD-ROM Living Books when you get more funding.

10. Set up the classroom. Enjoy learning with your students; witness the joy of daily writing. Welcome to the classroom of the twenty-first century.

Sample Software Reviews from Dr. Ann Lathrop's Software Clearinghouse

(http://www.stan–co.K12.ca.us)

The following pages contain a few samples of software reviews that can be obtained on the World Wide Web.

Kid Works 2

TITLE: Kid Works 2
RATING: Exemplary
SUBJECT: Art, English-Language Arts
PUBLISHER: Davidson & Associates, Inc.
GRADE LEVEL: K-4
TECHNOLOGY: Computer software
COMPUTER: IBM, Macintosh
STRATEGIES FOR ENGLISH LEARNERS: Yes
LANGUAGE: English, Spanish
MODE: Creative activity, Graphics generator, Instructional materials generator, Word processor
KEYWORDS: Composition, Creative activities, Drawing, Graphics, Painting, Reading, Sound, Vocabulary, Writing
PRICE: $89.95
COPYRIGHTED: 1991
YEAR EVALUATED: 1992

DESCRIPTION: This student creativity tool combines word processing, paint tools, and talking text. It is easy to use with on-screen menus. Students type in the text and draw their pictures. The program will read the text back to them. A picture dictionary allows the student to choose from pictures categorized as nouns, adjectives, and verbs. When a picture is added to their writing, the printed word is given with a click on the picture. The program helps students make connections between words and pictures, developing the link between writing and reading. Students who have used more powerful graphics programs may get frustrated, but it works well with the younger students for whom it was designed. Voice pronunciations are not always totally clear.

SUPPORT MATERIALS: There are 2 disks for IBM, 3 disks for Macintosh, and very thorough teacher's guide with many supporting ideas and lesson plans for the four unit themes.

SYSTEM REQUIREMENTS: An IBM with 640K and color monitor, or Macintosh with system 6.07 or higher is required. The Macintosh version of the program can be networked.

CURRICULUM APPLICATIONS: This program is highly motivating for the reluctant reader or writer who may need extra encouragement to become creative. After a simple demonstration of program capabilities, students can explore and create freely. Accompanying lessons direct students through the steps of the writing process. Cross-curricular applications are limitless as this tool can be used to communicate about any topic. The program is especially good for use with Special Education Students.

STRATEGIES FOR ENGLISH LEARNERS:
PRIMARY LANGUAGE INSTRUCTION: Spanish. All features of the program are available in Spanish.

ENGLISH LANGUAGE INSTRUCTION: KID WORKS 2 has several features that stand out as particularly useful with English learners. The text-to-speech feature allows the program to read back to the students anything they write; menu icons make it easy to navigate the program; text-to-pictures and pictures-to-text features facilitate understanding. The program is creative, open-ended, and highly motivating for younger and at-risk students because it very effectively uses the modalities of sight and sound. Students are able to combine graphics and text, and then record/playback their writing in their own voice or listen as their stories are read back to them by a classmate. The synthesized speech feature allows for pronunciation changes.

The iconmaker allows students to create their own icons with words they type and then record their own voices saying the words. This can be done in the primary language of the student as well as in English, although accent marks may not be available for all languages. It's also easy to do "rebus" stories with this program. **AGE RANGE:** 4-9. **LANGUAGE ACQUISITION STAGE:** All.

CALIFORNIA INSTRUCTIONAL TECHNOLOGY CLEARINGHOUSE
© 1995 Stanislaus County Office of Education

Children's Writing and Publishing Center

TITLE: The Children's Writing and Publishing Center
RATING: Exemplary
SUBJECT: English-Language Arts
PUBLISHER: The Learning Company
GRADE LEVEL: 2-8
STRATEGIES FOR ENGLISH LEARNERS: Yes
TECHNOLOGY: Computer software
COMPUTER: Apple, IBM
LANGUAGE: English, Spanish
KEYWORDS: Creative activities, Desktop publishing, Graphics, Newsletters, Prewriting, Revising, Word processing, Writing
MODE: Creative activity, Desktop publishing, Word processor
PRICE: $89.95; $179.95-$189.95 for Lab Edition (5 computers for all platforms); $699.00 for Apple Network, IBM Novell Network, Site License
COPYRIGHTED: 1988
YEAR EVALUATED: 1991

DESCRIPTION: This program is an easy-to-use desktop publishing program for grades 2 and up. It is simple enough for second graders to learn and use on their own. Students and teachers can create newsletters, certificates, surveys, stories, and more. Publications can be enhanced with graphics and fonts and can be printed in color (using a color ribbon). Publications are limited to four pages, however. Students using the program are motivated to write and to go through all the steps in process writing as they enjoy the opportunity to produce attractively printed and illustrated work.

SUPPORT MATERIALS: A template disk contains student activities and sample classroom materials.

STRATEGIES FOR ENGLISH LEARNERS:
PRIMARY LANGUAGE INSTRUCTION: Spanish. A Spanish language version is available as THE BILINGUAL WRITING CENTER.
ENGLISH LANGUAGE INSTRUCTION: The easy to use and intuitive menus make this program accessible to English learners. When incorporating picture files or graphics, students can access the guide to the picture files if the name of the graphic is not known or is unfamiliar in English. The teacher or a bilingual buddy can demonstrate how to save files and print documents. **AGE RANGE:** 6-Adult. **LANGUAGE ACQUISITION STAGE:** All.

CALIFORNIA INSTRUCTIONAL TECHNOLOGY CLEARINGHOUSE
© 1995 Stanislaus County Office of Education

Just Grandma and Me

TITLE: Just Grandma and Me
RATING: Exemplary
SUBJECT: English-Language Arts, History-Social Science
PUBLISHER: Broderbund Software, Inc.
GRADE LEVEL: K-6
TECHNOLOGY: CD-ROM
COMPUTER: IBM, Macintosh
STRATEGIES FOR ENGLISH LEARNERS: Yes
LANGUAGE: English, Japanese, Spanish
KEYWORDS: Beaches, Grandparents, Humorous stories, Literature, Reading, Seashore, Swimming; Mayer, Mercer
PRICE: $79.95
COPYRIGHTED: 1992
YEAR EVALUATED: 1994

DESCRIPTION: This CD-ROM is based on the original book by Mercer Mayer. The "book" can be read to students in one of three languages: English, Spanish or Japanese. There are two modes of using the program. In the "Read to Me" mode, the student can listen as the complete story is read. The story is read in a natural, human voice, not robotic at all. In the "Let Me Play" mode, the student listens to the sentences on a page and then can explore the page by pointing and clicking on various objects to see animations and to hear sound effects or music. The user controls the interactions on each page and the pace at which the story is explored. The content is interesting and appropriate for elementary students.

SUPPORT MATERIALS: School edition includes one CD-ROM with both Macintosh and MPC versions on it, a copy of the original book, a user's guide, a 39-page teacher's guide, TIME OF WONDER by Robert McCloskey, and the Steck-Vaughn WRITING DICTIONARY. The teacher's guide includes two annotated bibliographies (grandparents, water enviroments); classroom activities for language arts, reading, writing, art, science, and math; and a series of blackline masters.

SYSTEM REQUIREMENTS: Macintosh LC or II series with 4 MB RAM; system 6.0.7 or higher; 256 color monitor, CD-ROM drive. IBM/Tandy 386 or higher with 4 MB RAM; Windows 3.0 with multimedia extensions or Windows 3.1 with MPC extensions; Super VGA monitor, sound blaster or compatible sound card, mouse, hard drive and CD-ROM drive.

CURRICULUM APPLICATIONS: These are highly motivating materials for beginning readers to discover and explore. It is an interesting way to introduce students to interacting with the computer and using a mouse. Students can write, draw, or dictate other adventures with Grandma, either individually or as a group. The program provides the basis for class discussions and writing opportunities about what adventures are, and what little events can happen between the major events.

STRATEGIES FOR ENGLISH LEARNERS:
PRIMARY LANGUAGE INSTRUCTION: Japanese, Spanish. Students can select any one of the three languages in which they wish to have the story read to them. The narrators are native speakers with authentic intonation. The Japanese written language is in all the forms used in Japan (Hiragana, Katakana, and Kanji) and the spoken language is representative of the Japanese culture; the inflection and tone are gentle and pleasing to the ear, and the humor is appealing. The interactive "Let Me Play" feature is also presented in the language selected.

ENGLISH LANGUAGE INSTRUCTION: The program appears to promote effective language development experiences. The students observed using the program were engaging in lively discussions, predicting outcomes, reading the text before it was read to them, and sharing personal experiences related to the theme. **AGE RANGE:** 5-9. **LANGUAGE ACQUISITION STAGE:** All.

CALIFORNIA INSTRUCTIONAL TECHNOLOGY CLEARINGHOUSE
© 1995 Stanislaus County Office of Education

Appendix G

Early Literacy and Technology Resources

Professional Associations, Conferences, and Journals Dealing with Early Literacy or Technology

American Montessori Society, Inc. (AMS), 150 Fifth Avenue, New York, NY 10010.

Association for Childhood Education International (ACEI), 11141 Georgia Avenue, Ste. 200, Wheaton, MD 20902. Journal: *Childhood Education.*

Children's Bureau, Office of Child Development, U.S. Department of Health, Education and Welfare, Washington, DC 20201. Journal: *Children Today.*

Closing the Gap, P.O. Box 68, Henderson, MN 56044. Conference: Microcomputer Technology for Special Education and Rehabilitiation Conference, held each fall in Minneapolis, MN. Journal: *Closing the Gap.*

Computer Using Educators, 1210 Marina Village Parkway, Suite 100, Alameda, CA 94501; cueinc@aol.com. Newsletter: *CUE Newsletter.*

Educational Resource Information Center/Early Childhood Education (ERIC/ECE), University of Illinois, 804 West Pennsylvania Avenue, Urbana, IL 61801.

Highlights for Children, Inc., P.O. Box 1266, Darien, CT 06820. Journal: *Early Years.*

International Reading Association (IRA), 800 Barksdale Road, P.O. Box 8139, Newark, DE 19711. Journals: *Reading Teacher; Reading Research Quarterly.*

International Society for Technology in Education (ISTE), 1787 Agate Street, Eugene, OR 97403. Journal: *Learning & Leading with Technology* (Formerly *The Computing Teacher*).

Multimedia Schools, 462 Danbury Road, Wilton, CT 06897-9819. Journal: *Multimedia Schools.*

National Association for the Education of Young Children (NAEYC), 1834 Connecticut Avenue NW, Washington, DC 20009. Journal: *Young Children.*

National Council of Teachers of English (NCTE), 111 Kenyon Road, Urbana, IL 61801. Journal: *Language Arts.*

National Reading Conference (NRC), 1070 Sibley Tower, Rochester, NY 14604. Journal: *Journal of Reading Behavior.*

Scholastic, Inc., 730 Broadway, New York, NY 10012. Journal: *Electronic Learning.*

Review Sources Online

Educators and parents should check these sources for reviews of children's reading and language arts software.

California Instructional Technology Clearinghouse
801 County Center 3 Court
Modesto, CA 95355-4490
http://www.stan-co.k12.ca.us
209-525-4900

Computer Database
Information Access Company
362 Lakeside Drive
Foster City, CA 94404
DIALOG Database #275
800-321-6388

Language On-Line
Knowledge Computing
9 Ashdown Drive
Borehamwood, Herts. WD64LZ United Kingdom
http://www.knowledge.co.uk/xxx/
44-181-953-7722

Rainbo Electronic Reviews
8 Duran Street
Pacifica, CA 94044
GENIE
800-638-9636

Software Reviews by Educators, for Educators
Learning Center
eWorld Educator Connection
eWorld
800-521-1515

Bibliography

Allington, R., and P. Cunningham. 1996. *Schools That Work: Where All Children Read and Write*. New York: HarperCollins.

Anderson, R. C., E. Heibert, J. Scott, and I. Wilkinson. 1985. *Becoming a Nation of Readers: The Report of the Commission on Reading*. Washington, DC: National Institute of Education.

Armstrong, Thomas. 1995. *The Myth of the ADD Child: 50 Ways to Improve Your Child's Attention Span Without Drugs, Labels, or Coercion*. New York: Dutton.

Au, Kathryn H. 1993. *Literacy Instruction in Multicultural Settings*. Fort Worth, TX: Harcourt Brace.

Baghban, Marcia. 1984. *Our Daughter Learns to Read and Write*. Newark, DE: International Reading Association.

Balajthy, Ernest. 1986. *Microcomputers in Reading and Language Arts*. Englewood Cliffs, NJ: Prentice-Hall.

Barbour, A. 1987. "Computerized Speech: Talking Its Way into the Classroom." *Electronic Learning* 6:4(January):15–16.

Barriere, M., and C. Plaisant. 1986. "Quelques Effets de l'Expérimentation sur la Realisation et le Développment de Logiciels de Sensibilisation à la Langue Ecrite." *Les Amis de Sevres (C.I.E.P.)* No. 2.

Begley, Sharon. 1996. "Your Child's Brain." *Newsweek* (February 19):54–61.

Bilotti, Lawrence. 1996. Home Office Solutions. Hearst Corp. (www.homearts.com).

Bissex, Glenda L. 1980. *Gnys at Wrk: A Child Learns to Write and Read*. Cambridge, MA: Harvard Univ. Press.

Bloom, B. 1964. *Stability and Change in Human Characteristics*. New York: John Wiley.

Boehm, Diann. 1993. "Creative Writing at Its Best with Kid Works 2." *The Writing Notebook* 10(April/May):13–14.

Bond, G. L., and R. Dykstra. 1967. "The Cooperative Research Program in First-Grade Reading Instruction." *Reading Research Quarterly* 2:5–142.

Borgh, K., and P. Dickson. 1992. "The Effects on Children's Writing of Adding Speech Synthesis to a Word Processor." *Journal of Research on Computing in Education* 5:46–56.

Boyer, Ernest L. 1995. *The Basic School: A Community for Learning*. Princeton, NJ: Carnegie Foundation.

Brand, Steward. 1987. *The Media Lab*. New York: Viking.

Brierley, Mirian. 1987. *Writing to Read and Full Day Kindergarten*. Columbus, OH: Columbus Public Schools, Dept. of Evaluation Services. ED 289 626.

Brooks, D. M., and T. W. Kopp. 1989. "Technology in Teacher Education." *Journal of Teacher Education* 4:2–8.

Bull, G., J. Harris, J. Lloyd, and J. Short. 1989. "The Electronic Academic Village." *Journal of Teacher Education* 4:27–31.

Byars, Betsy. 1970. *Summer of the Swans*. New York: Viking Press.

Calkins, Lucy M. 1991. *Living Between the Lines*. New York: Heinemann.

———. 1986. *The Art of Teaching Writing*. Portsmouth, NH: Heinemann.

———. 1983. *Lessons from a Child: On the Teaching and Learning of Writing*. Exeter, NH: Heinemann.

Cambourne, B. 1988. *The Whole Story: Natural Learning and the Acquisition of Literacy in the Classroom*. Richmond-Hill, ON: Scholastic-TAB.

Casey, Chris. 1996. *The Hill on the Net: Congress Enters the Information Age*. San Diego, CA: Academic Press.

Casey, Jean. 1994a. "Literacy Instruction in an Integrated Curriculum." *The Computing Teacher* 21:5(February):33–37.

———. 1992a. *Simi Star Project Report*. Long Beach: California State University, Long Beach.

———. 1991. "The Language Machine: Technology Can Be a Ticket for Entry into the Literacy Club." *The California Reader* 24:4:12–15.

———. 1990. "Using Computers with Problem Readers." In *Hi/Low Handbook*, edited by E. Libretto. New York: Bowker.

———. 1985. "Making Micros Talk." *Electronic Learning* 10(October):16, 21–22.

———. 1984. "A Descriptive Study of a School District's Reading Program." Ph.D. diss., University of Southern California.

Casey, Jean, and Mary Cron. 1983. KidTalk. Long Beach, CA: First Byte.

Casey, J. M., and R. A. Roth. 1992b. "An Impact Analysis of Technology-Based Support in Student Teaching." *Teacher Education and Practice* (Fall/Winter):23– .

Chall, Jeanne S. 1983. *Learning to Read: The Great Debate*. New York: McGraw-Hill.

Chandler, D., and S. Marcus, eds. 1985. *Computers and Literacy*. Philadelphia: Open University Press.

Chomsky, C. 1978. "When You Still Can't Read in Third Grade: After Decoding, What?" In *What Research Has to Say About Reading Instruction*, edited by S. J. Samuels. Newark, DE: International Reading Association.

Clay, Marie M. 1991. *Becoming Literate: The Construction of Inner Control*. Portsmouth, NH: Heinemann.

Clements, D. 1987. "Computers and Young Children: A Review of Research." *Young Children* (November):34–44.

———. 1985. *Computers in Early and Primary Education*. Englewood Cliffs, NJ: Prentice-Hall.

Clinton, Hillary R. 1996. *It Takes a Village: And Other Lessons Children Teach Us*. New York: Simon & Schuster.

Cochran-Smith, M., J. Kakhn, and C. Paris. 1988. "When Word Processors Come into the Classroom." In *Writing with Computers in the Early Grades*, edited by J. Hoot and S. Silvern, 143–159. New York: Teachers College Press.

Cohen, Rachel. 1995. *La communication telematique internationale, une mutation dans l'education*. Paris: Retz-Nathan.

———. 1993. "The Use of Voice Synthesizer in the Discovery of the Written Language by Young Children." *Computers Education, Great Britain* 21:6:25–30.

———. 1992a. *Quand l'ordinateur parle …, Utilisation de la synthese vocale dans l'apprentissage et le perfectionnement de la langue ecrite*. Paris: Presses Universitaires de France.

———. 1992b. "The Use of Voice Synthesizer in the Discovery of the Written Language by Very Young Children." *ECER–University of Twente* (June):20–30.

———. 1988. "One Computer, Two Languages, Many Children: Helping Non-Francophone Children to Integrate into French Classrooms." *Education and Computing* 4:145–149.

———. 1982. *Plaidoyer pour les Apprentissages Précoces*. Paris: Presses Universitaires de France.

———. 1977. *L'Apprentissage Précoce de la Lecture*. Paris: Presses Universitaires de France.

Cohen, R., M. Barriere, C. Halfter, J. Naymark, C. Plaisant, and C. Stambak. 1987. *Les jeunes enfants, la Découverte de l'Ecrit et l'Ordinateur*. Paris: Presses Universitaires de France.

Cohen, R., et al. 1992. *Quand l'ordinateur parle …* Paris: Presses Universitaires de France.

————. 1989. "Que sont-ils devenus? Les effets des apprentissages précoces." *Revue Francaise de Pedagogie (Institut National de Recherche Pèdagogique)* 88:27–41.

Cohen, R., and H. Gilabert. 1988b. *Découverte et Apprentissage du langage ecrit Avant 6 Ans.* 2d ed. Paris: Presses Universitaires de France.

Coles, Gerald. 1987. *The Learning Mystique.* New York: Pantheon Books.

Cooper, J. David. 1993. *Literacy: Helping Children Construct Meaning.* New York: Houghton Mifflin.

Costanzo, W. 1994. "Reading, Writing, and Thinking in an Age of Electronic Literacy." In *Literacy and Computers: The Complications of Teaching and Learning with Technology,* edited by Cynthia L. Selfe and Susan Hilligoss. New York: Modern Language Association.

Cummins, Jim, and Dennis Sayers. 1995. *Brave New Schools: Challenging Cultural Illiteracy Through Global Learning Networks.* New York: St. Martin's Press.

Dahl, I. 1990. "Listen to Learn How to Read and Write with Computer and Speech Output: Experiences and Results." In *13th World Congress on Reading, IRA in Stockholm.* Newark, DE: International Reading Association.

DeAmbrose, E., et al. 1991. "Turned on to Technology." *Instructor* 101:30–36.

Deboe, M., and others. 1984. *Writing to Read in the Portland, Oregon, Public Schools.* Portland Public Schools. ED 255 552.

DeFord, D. E., C. A. Lyons, and G. S. Pinnell. 1991. *Bridges to Literacy: Learning from Reading Recovery.* Portsmouth, NH: Heinemann.

Dion, R. 1988. "Team Teaching with a Talking Computer." *The Computing Teacher* (March):16–18.

Dulay, H., and M. Burt. 1973. "Should We Teach Syntax?" *Language Learning* 23:2(December):245–58.

Durkin, Delores. 1966. *Children Who Read Early.* New York: Teachers College Press.

Emig, Janet. 1983. "Non-Magical Thinking: Presenting Writing Developmentally in Schools." In *The Web of Meaning.* Portsmouth, NH: Boynton-Cook/Heinemann.

Evans, Paul. 1988. "The Corporate Kindergarten: Writing to Read." *Journal of the Pi Lambda Theta International Honor Society and Professional Association in Education* (Summer:160–63).

Fernald, G. M. 1943. *Remedial Techniques in Basic School Subjects.* New York: McGraw-Hill.

Ferreiro, E. 1986. "Literacy Development: Psychogenesis." In *IRA 11th World Congress in London.* Newark, DE: International Reading Association.

Ferreiro, E., and A. Teberosky. 1989. *Literacy Before Schooling.* Portsmouth, NH: Heinemann.

Flesch, Rudolf. 1955. *Why Johnny Can't Read and What You Can Do About It*. New York: Harper & Brothers.

Galda, L., B. Cullinan, and D. Strickland. 1993. *Language, Literacy and the Child*. New York: Harcourt Brace Jovanovich.

Gates, Bill. 1995. *The Road Ahead*. New York: Viking Press.

Gesell, Arnold. 1940. *The First Five Years of Life*. New York: Harper & Brothers.

Gesell, Arnold, and Frances Ilg. 1946. *The Child from Five to Ten*. New York: Harper & Brothers.

Gipe, J., C. Duffy, and J. Richards. 1993. "Helping a Nonspeaking Adult Male with Cerebral Palsy Achieve Literacy." In *Adult Literacy*, edited by Marguerite Radencich. Newark, DE: International Reading Association.

Gonzalez-Baker, Maria. 1989. *A Guide for Teaching English as a Second Language: Using Technology*. Atlanta, GA: IBM. 1ATL37.3046.1C.1.

———. 1986. "Spanish Literacy Series (SABES and SESOS)." San Antonio, TX: P. Falcon International.

Goodlad, John I. 1984. *A Place Called School*. New York: McGraw-Hill.

Goodman, K. S. 1986. *What's Whole in Whole Language*. Portsmouth, NH: Heinemann.

Goodman, Yetta, ed. 1990. *How Children Construct Literacy: Piagetian Perspectives*. Newark, DE: International Reading Association.

Gould, Stephen Jay. 1981. *The Mismeasure of Man*. New York: Norton.

Graves, Donald H. 1994. "Be a Better Writing Teacher." *Instructor* (November/ December):43–46.

———. 1983. *Writing: Teachers and Children at Work*. Portsmouth, NH: Heinemann.

Greenleaf, Cynthia. 1992. Technological Indeterminancy: The Role of Classroom Writing Practices in Shaping Computer Use. Center for the Study of Writing and Literacy. Technical Report No. 57.

Griffith, P. L., J. P. Kesius, and J. D. Kromrey. 1992. "The Effects of Phonemic Awareness in the Literacy Development of First Grade Children in a Traditional and Whole Language Classroom." *Journal of Research in Childhood Education* (Spring/Summer):85–92.

Grimm, E. 1988. "Coming on Fast in the Classroom." *Think: The IBM Magazine* 54:5–8.

Guthrie, L., and S. Richardson. 1995. "Computer Literacy in the Primary Grades." *Educational Leadership* 53:2:14–16.

Guyton, E., and J. D. McIntyre. 1990. "Student Teaching and School Experiences." In *Handbook of Research on Teacher Education*, edited by R. W. Houston, M. Haberman, and J. Sikula. 514–531. New York: Macmillan.

Hakuta, Kenji. 1986. *Mirror of Language: The Debate on Bilingualism*. New York: Basic Books.

Hamm-Schwartz, Deborah. 1996. Personal communication.

Harvey, W. 1983. "Voice Synthesis: A New Technology Comes to School." *Electronic Learning* 5(February):68–73.

Heath, Shirley Brice. 1983. *Ways with Words: Language, Life and Work in Communities and Classrooms*. Cambridge: Cambridge Univ. Press.

Heller, Mary F. 1991. *Reading–Writing Connections: From Theory to Practice*. New York: Longman.

Hess, R. D. 1986. "Effects of Microcomputer Use in Kindergarten on Students' Social Behavior and Academic Performance." *AERA* (April):251–261.

Hiebert, E., and B. Taylor. 1994. *Getting Reading Right from the Start*. Boston: Allyn and Bacon.

Holdaway, Don. 1979. *Foundations of Literacy*. Sydney, Australia: Ashton Scholastic.

Holzberg, Carol S. 1990. "Watch Kids Get Excited." *Today's Catholic Teacher* (September Supplement):1–20.

Howie, Sherry. 1994. "Adult Literacy in a Multiliterate Society." In *Adult Literacy: A Compendium of Articles from the Journal of Reading*, edited by Marguerite Radencich, 181–185. Newark, DE: International Reading Association.

Hutchins, Pat. 1968. *Rosie's Walk*. New York: Macmillan.

Inhelder, B., and G. Céllerier. 1992. *Le cheminement des découvertes de l'enfant*. Lausanne: Delachaux et Niestlé.

Jacquard, A. 1978. *Eloge de la Différence. La Génétique et les Hommes*. Paris: Seuil.

Juel, C. 1988. "Learning to Read and Write: A Longitudinal Study of 54 Children From First and Second Grade." *Journal of Educational Psychology* 80:4:437–447.

Juster, Norton. 1961. *The Phantom Toll Booth*. New York: Epstein & Carroll.

Karelitz, Ellen B. 1993. *The Author's Chair and Beyond: Language and Literacy in the Primary Classroom*. Portsmouth, NH: Heinemann.

Kozol, Jonathan. 1985. *Illiterate America*. New York: Anchor Press/Doubleday.

Krashen, Stephen. 1993. *The Power of Reading*. Englewood, CO: Libraries Unlimited.

———. 1985. *Inquiries and Insights*. Haywood, CA: Almenay Press.

———. 1984. *Writing, Research, Theory and Application*. Oxford: Pergamon.

———. 1981. *Second Language Acquisition and Second Language Learning*. Oxford: Pergamon.

Labbo, L., B. Murray, and M. Phillips. 1995. "Writing to Read: From Inheritance to Innovation and Invitation." *The Reading Teacher* 499:4 (December 1995/January 1996):314–321.

Lathrop, Ann. 1995. "California Instructional Technology Clearinghouse." Modesto, CA: Stanislaus County Office of Education.

Lawler, R. W. 1985. *Computer Experience and Cognitive Development: A Child's Learning in a Computer Culture*. Chichester, England: Ellis Horwood.

Lomax, R. G., and L. M. McGee. 1987. "Young Children's Concepts about Print and Reading: Toward a Model of Word Reading Acquisition." *Reading Research Quarterly* 22:2(Spring):237–56.

Lundberg, I., J. Frost, and O. Peterson. 1988. "Effects of an Extensive Program for Stimulating Phonological Awareness in Preschool Children." *Reading Research Quarterly* 23:3:263–84.

Lurçat, L. 1985. *l'Ecriture et le Langage Ecrit de l'Enfant*. Paris: Editions Sociales Francaises.

Male, Mary. 1994. *Technology for Inclusion: Meeting the Special Needs of all Students*. Boston: Allyn & Bacon.

Martin, John Henry. 1993. JHM Corp. "Writing to Read 2000." Atlanta, GA: IBM.

Martin, J. H., and A. Friedberg. 1986. *Writing to Read*. New York: Warner Books.

Mason, G. 1986. "The New Speaking Programs." *The Reading Teacher* 39:6(February):618–20.

Mazurkiewicz, Albert J. 1964. "Teaching Reading in America Using the Initial Teaching Alphabet." *Elementary English* 41:7:776– .

Meirieu, Ph. 1991. *Apprendre ... oui mais comment*. 8th ed. Paris: E.S.F.

Meyers, Laura. 1984. "Unique Contributions of Microcomputers to Language Intervention with Handicapped Children." *Seminars in Speech and Language* 5:1(February):23–33.

Moore, G. R. 1993. "Computer to Computer: Mentoring Possibilities." *Educational Leadership* 50:1(January):43–53.

Moore, O. K. 1961. "Orthographic Symbols and the Preschool Child—a New Approach." In *Third Minnesota Conference on Gifted Children*. Minnesota Center for Continuation Study, University of Minnesota, 91–101.

Morphett, Mabel V., and C. Washburn. 1931. "When Should Children Begin to Read?" *Elementary School Journal* 31:3:496–503.

Morrow, Lesley M. 1989. *Literacy Development in the Early Years: Helping Children Read and Write*. Englewood Cliffs, NJ: Prentice-Hall.

———, ed. 1995. *Family Literacy*. Newark, DE: International Reading Association.

Naron, Nancy K. 1986. *Writing to Read Program, 1985–86*. Fort Worth, TX: Fort Worth Independent School District and Texas Dept. of Research and Evaluation. ED 283 843.

Naymark, J., and C. Plaisant. 1986. *The Computers and the Preschool Child: The Written Language and Play*. London: Pergamon.

Negroponte, Nicholas. 1995. *being digital*. New York: Alfred A. Knopf.

Olofsson, A. 1988. *Phonemic Awareness and the Use of Computer Speech in Reading Remediation: Theoretical Background*. Fonetiks.

Olson, R., G. Roltz, and B. Wise. 1984. "Behavior Research Methods, Instruments, and Computers." *Journal of the Psychonomic Society* 16:1.

Olson, R. K., and B. Wise. 1987. "Computer Speech in Reading Instruction." In *Computers and Reading Issues for Theory and Practice*, edited by D. Reiking. New York: Teachers College Press, Columbia University.

Ovando, C., and V. Collier. 1985. *Bilingual and ESL Classrooms*. New York: McGraw-Hill.

Papert, Seymour. 1993. *The Children's Machine: Rethinking School in the Age of the Computer*. New York: Basic Books.

———. 1980. *Mindstorms: Children, Computers and Powerful Ideas*. New York: Basic Books.

Parham, Charles. 1988. "Computers That Talk." *Classroom Computer Learning* (March):26–31.

Perelman, L. J. 1992. *School's Out: Hyperlearning, the New Technology, and the End of Education*. New York: William Morrow.

Perkins, W., ed. 1984. Seminar in Language: "Use of Microcomputers to Remediate Speech Through Literacy." Conference proceedings, American Speech Language and Hearing Association. Rockville, MD: American Speech Language and Hearing Association.

Pezoldt, Connie. 1989. "A Cross-Case Analysis of the Implementation of Writing to Read." Fullerton: California State University, Fullerton.

Piazza, C., and S. Riggs. 1984. "Writing with a Computer: An Invitation to Play." *Early Child Development & Care* 17:13:63–76.

Pitman, Sir James. 1963. "The Future of the Teaching Reading." Paper presented at the Educational Conference of the Educational Records Bureau, New York, October 30–November 1, 1963.

Postman, N. 1992. *Technopoly: The Surrender of Culture to Technology*. New York: Alfred A. Knopf.

Programmes ALE. 1987. Paris: Jeriko.

Pyle, Amy. 1996. "L.A. Parents Say Bilingual Classes Failing." *Los Angeles Times*, (January 16):1,8.

Public Broadcasting System. 1994. "Children and Computers." *No*

Radencich, Marguerite C., ed. 1994. *Adult Literacy*. Newark, DE: Inter Association.

Reinking, Ian D., ed. 1986. *Computer and Reading: Issues for Theory and Practi* York: Teachers College Press.

Reitsma, Pieter. 1988. "Reading Practice for Beginners: Effects of Guided Reading, Reading-While-Listening, and Independent Reading with Computer-Based Speech Feedback." *Reading Research Quarterly* 23:12:219–35.

Robinson, R., M. McKenna, and J. Wedman. 1996. *Issues and Trends in Literacy Education*. Boston: Allyn & Bacon.

Rosegrant, T. J., and R. A. Cooper. 1983. *The Talking Screen Textwriter*. Phoenix, AZ: Computing Adventures.

Scollon, S. B., and R. Scollon. 1984. "Run Trilogy: Can Tommy Read?" In *Awakening to Literacy*, edited by H. Goelman, A. Oberg, and F. Smith. 131–40. Exeter, NH: Heinemann.

Selfe, C. L., and S. Hilligoss, ed. 1994 *Literacy and Computers: The Complications of Teaching and Learning with Technology*. New York: Modern Language Association.

Sendak, Maurice. 1963. *Where the Wild Things Are*. New York: Harper & Row.

Shade, D. D., and J. A. Watson. 1990. "Computers in Early Education: Issues Put to Rest, Theoretical Links to Sound Practice, and the Potential Contribution of Microworlds." *Journal of Educational Computing Research* 6:4:375–92.

Silverstein, Shel. 1974. *Where the Sidewalk Ends*. New York: Harper & Row.

Slavin, R. 1990. "IBM's Writing to Read." *Phi Delta Kappan* 72:3(November):214–16.

Smith, Carl B. 1994. *Whole Language: The Debate*. Bloomington, IN: ERIC Press.

Smith, Frank. 1990. *to think*. Columbia, New York: Teachers College Press.

———. 1988a. *Joining the Literacy Club: Further Essays into Education*. Portsmouth, NH: Heinemann.

———. 1988b. *Understanding Reading*. Hillsdale, NJ: Lawrence Erlbaum.

———. 1984. *The Promise and Threat of Microcomputers in Language Education*. Victoria, BC: Able Press.

———. 1983. *Essays into Literacy*. Exeter, NH: Heinemann.

Snow, C. 1991. "The Theoretical Basis for Relationships Between Language and Literacy in Development." *Journal of Research in Childhood Education* 6 (Fall/Winter):5–10.

Stahl, S. A., and P. Miller. 1989. "Whole Language and Language Experience: Approaches for Beginning Reading: A Qualitative Research Synthesis." *Review of Educational Research* 59:3:87–116.

ernative to Word Processing—FrEdWriter."

ad." In *U.S.C. Reading Conference in U.S.C.* University Publications.

n the Use of Technology in Teacher *tion* 40:4:33–35.

ee Cs: Children, Computers, and Communication.

1987. *Using Computers in the Teaching of* ss.

Sulzby, Elizabeth. 1994. "Write Along." *IBM-Eduquest.*

Taylor, Denny. 1993. *From a Child's Point of View.* Portsmouth, NH: Heinemann.

———. 1991. *Learning Denied.* Portsmouth, NH: Heinemann.

———. 1983. *Family Literacy.* Portsmouth, NH: Heinemann.

Taylor, Denny, and Catherine Dorsey-Gaines. 1988. *Growing up Literate: Learning from Inner-City Families.* Portsmouth, NH: Heinemann.

Teale, William H., and Elizabeth Sulzby, ed. 1986. *Emergent Literacy: Writing and Reading.* Norwood, NJ: Ablex Publishing.

Turkle, S. 1984. *The Second Self: Computers and the Human Spirit.* New York: Simon & Schuster.

U.S. Department of Education, National Center for Education Statistics. 1995. NAEP Reading: A First Look, May 1995.

Van Allen, R. 1976. *Language Experience and Communication.* Boston: Houghton Mifflin.

Veatch, Jeanette. 1959. *Individualizing Your Reading Program.* New York: G. P. Putnam's Sons.

Warner, Sylvia Ashton. 1986. *Teacher.* New York: Simon & Schuster.

Webb, J., E. Meckstroth, and S. Tolan. 1982. *Guiding the Gifted Child.* Columbus, OH: Ohio Psychology Publishing.

Wells, Gordon. 1986. *The Meaning Makers: Children Learning Language and Using Language to Learn.* Portsmouth, NH: Heinemann.

White, E. B. 1952. *Charlotte's Web.* New York: Harper & Row.

Winner, L. 1994. "The Virtually Educated." *Technology Review* (May/June):66.

Index

About the Author and Contributors

Dr. Jean M. Casey is one of the pioneer researchers in computers with speech for early literacy development. She completed her Ph.D. at the University of Southern California in 1984. She has continued to work with young children and the empowerment technology can bring to their early literacy development. She was the author of the software program known as KidTalk, which was the first talking word processor with the speech resident on the disk. A revised, updated version of KidTalk is now known as KidWorks 2. Dr. Casey was also the evaluator of the 24-classroom, 6 school district Simi Star Project. In this she evaluated more than 1,000 writing samples by five and six year olds. She is a noted lecturer in this field and has spoken throughout the United States, Australia, and Europe on this topic. She also created TeacherNet, the first west coast program of telecommunications for student teachers, master teachers, and university supervisors. In early 1996, Dr. Casey was featured on the BeachTalk cable TV show; her work in technology, early literacy and teacher education was highlighted. Copies of this show are available from: CSULB ITV, 1250 S. Bellflower Blvd., Long Beach, CA 90840.

Dr. Rachel Cohen is a well-known European educational leader. A full-time researcher at the University Paris-Nord, she has served as Director of Ecole Active Bilingue, the International School of Paris, and she created an experimental Teacher Training College. Her research interests include early childhood education (with special emphasis on early learning as a means against illiteracy and school failure), multilingualism and international education, teacher training, and new technologies in communication and information. She is the author of seven books about young children and technology. These have been translated into many languages. She has also written a great number of articles in scientific international journals.

Dr. Gloria Medrano is a noted researcher in early education and the computer in Spain. She and her colleague, Dr. Maria Luisa Herrero Nivela, are researchers in the Department of Psychology and Sociology at the University of Zaragoza in Spain.

Dr. Maria Gonzalez-Baker is a respected Hispanic researcher and educator who has worked with Spanish and ESL youngsters in Texas, Puerto Rico, and the western United States. She has created the SABES and SESOS Spanish Early Literacy Programs.

All of the researchers started out as early childhood classroom teachers. Their love of that age group and their determination to find the environment in which all children learn to write and read regardless of language, country, socioeconomic status, or special need, has motivated them to join forces in bringing this important message to educators everywhere.